Standard Grade | General | Credit

Computing Studies

General Level 2001

Credit Level 2001

General Level 2002

Credit Level 2002

General Level 2003

Credit Level 2003

General Level 2004

Credit Level 2004

General Level 2005

Credit Level 2005

First exam published in 2001.

Published by Leckie & Leckie, 8 Whitehill Terrace, St. Andrews, Scotland KY16 8RN tel: 01334 475656 fax: 01334 477392 enquiries@leckieandleckie.co.uk www.leckieandleckie.co.uk

ISBN 1-84372-294-1

A CIP Catalogue record for this book is available from the British Library.

Printed in Scotland by Scotprint.

Leckie & Leckie is a division of Granada Learning Limited, part of ITV plc.

Acknowledgements

Leckie & Leckie is grateful to the copyright holders, as credited at the back of the book, for permission to use their material.

Every effort has been made to trace the copyright holders and to obtain their permission to use their copyright material.

Leckie & Leckie will gladly receive information enabling them to rectify any error or omission in subsequent editions.

[BLANK PAGE]

FOR OFFICIAL USE

G

KU   PS

Total Marks

0560/402

NATIONAL
QUALIFICATIONS
2001

TUESDAY, 5 JUNE
G/C 9.00 AM – 10.15 AM
F/G 10.20 AM – 11.35 AM

**COMPUTING STUDIES
STANDARD GRADE**
General Level

Fill in these boxes and read what is printed below.

Full name of centre

Town

Forename(s)

Surname

Date of birth
Day Month Year

Scottish candidate number

Number of seat

Read each question carefully.

Attempt **all** questions.

Write your answers in the space provided on the question paper.

Write as neatly as possible.

Answer in sentences wherever possible.

Before leaving the examination room you must give this book to the invigilator. If you do not, you may lose all the marks for this paper.

SCOTTISH
QUALIFICATIONS
AUTHORITY

©

1. Gemma is to have a party. She starts making invitations by having an arrow shaped graphic and some text as shown in the first draft. She makes some changes and produces a second draft as shown.

First draft	**Second draft**
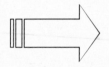	
Gemma's birthday party You are invited to come to my Party Be there or miss the big one!!	**Gemma's birthday party** **You are invited to come to my Party** **Be there or miss the big one!!**
Date: 24 February Venue: Laser Vision Club Time: 8.00 pm to midnight RSVP: 0191 234 567	Date: 24 February Venue: Laser Vision Club Time: 8.00 pm to midnight RSVP: 0191 234 567

(a) The arrow graphic has been copied and used twice. The one at the top of the second draft has been placed in the centre of the page. State **two** other ways in which this graphic has been edited from the original one shown in the first draft.

1 _____

_____

2 _____

_____

2
1
0

(b) The first three lines of text have been centred. State **two** other changes that have been made to that text.

1 _____

_____

2 _____

_____

2
1
0

(c) The alignment has been changed for the last four lines of text in the second draft. List the **two** steps required to do this.

1 _____

_____

2 _____

_____

(d) (i) Gemma wishes to print out her invitations but only has a dot matrix printer.

Explain why she might not want to use her dot matrix printer for her invitations.

_____

_____

(ii) Gemma has to choose between buying an ink jet printer and a laser printer.

Give **one** reason why she might decide to buy the ink jet printer.

_____

_____

(e) Gemma uses an *integrated package* with a *graphical user interface* to produce her invitations. What is meant by:

(i) integrated package;

_____

_____

_____

(ii) graphical user interface?

_____

_____

_____

[Turn over

1. **(continued)**

   (*f*) The package has *on-line help* and *on-line tutorials*. If she forgets how to edit a graphic, which of these **two** features would she use to overcome her problem?

   _____

   Explain your answer.

   _____

   _____

Page four

[Turn over for Question 2 on *Page six*

KU | PS

2. Helen keeps track of her monthly finances using a spreadsheet as shown below.

	A	B	C	D	E	F
1	**Date of month**	**Monthly expenses**	**Amount**		**Income**	**Amount**
2	1	Golf fees	50.50			
3	1	Mortgage	295.00			
4	5	Insurance	36.40		Wages	1600.00
5	12	Gas	34.00		Child allowance	150.00
6	12	Electricity	23.00			
7	15	Phone	18.20			
8	23	Car loan	325.00			
9	28	Council tax	50.00			
10						
11		**Other expenses**				
12		Food	300.00			
13		Car petrol/servicing	120.00			
14		Child minder	160.00			
15						
16		**Total expenses**	£ 1,412.10		**Total income**	£ 1,750.00
17						
18		Spare each month	£ 337.90			
19						

(a) The amount for golf fees appeared as 50.5 originally. What has Helen done to change the way it looks in the spreadsheet?

_____

1
0

(b) In what way is the format of cell C16 different from the format of the cell C2?

_____

1
0

(c) State the formula which goes in cell C18.

_____

1
0

(d) The formula in cell C16 has been entered as
=C2+C3+C4+C5+C6+C7+C8+C9+C10+C11+C12+C13+C14

Write this in a shorter form.

_____

1
0

(e)   (i)   Helen buys some bedroom furniture and takes out a loan to pay for it. Her monthly payment will be £60 and will be due on the 14th day of the month.

What will Helen do to include this on her spreadsheet?

_____

_____

_____

(ii)   Helen wants to put the words "Bedroom furniture loan" under the Monthly expenses heading but it will not fit. How can she alter the sheet to make this possible?

_____

_____

[Turn over

3. The Computing Department of St Cecelia's High School has three computing rooms which are all networked together within the school.

(a) State the name of this type of computer network.

_____

(b) (i) The network requires both *backing store* and *backup*. Explain what is meant by each of these terms.

Backing store _____

_____

Backup _____

_____

(ii) One of the networked computers has a floppy disc drive, CD ROM drive (read only), magnetic tape drive and hard disc drive.

Which **one** of the following would you recommend as backing storage medium? Choose your answer from the list below and give a reason for your choice.

Floppy disc   *CD ROM*   *Magnetic tape*   *Hard disc*

Backing store medium _____

Reason _____

_____

(iii) Pick **one** of the other media from the list and explain why it would not be suitable for backing storage.

_____

_____

(c) The school holds large amounts of data about staff and pupils on computer. State **two** precautions the school must take to protect the data.

_____

_____

_____

KU	PS
10	
210	
	20
	210
210	

(d) Next year, pupils will be able to access their files, stored at school, from their own computer at home. Which additional piece of hardware will be needed for this?

_____

1
0

[Turn over

4. A database containing details of a school's list of penfriends is shown below.

Forename	Surname	Age	Sex	Town/City	Interest
Alain	Pilot	11	M	Alsace	Soccer
Lola	Himinez	12	F	Barcelona	Golf
Jack	Deleaney	14	M	Dublin	Pop music
Mairi	Bellamy	15	F	London	Cooking
David	Jones	13	M	Birmingham	Golf
Miguel	Garcia	12	M	Madrid	Soccer
Tina	Ferez	10	F	Valencia	Pop music
Roisin	McShane	14	F	Belfast	Martial arts
Stephan	Gerard	13	M	Lyon	Pop music
Jasmine	Defritas	15	F	Bologna	Aerobics
Didier	Champagne	12	M	Paris	Swimming
Virginie	Desaille	15	F	Paris	Aerobics
Lindsay	Wagner	11	F	Berlin	Soccer
Suzanne	Winters	12	F	Glasgow	Dancing

(*a*) Describe how you would use the database to find the following information.

(i) A list with the youngest to the oldest in order.

_____

_____

_____

2
1
0

(ii) A list of boys in the database aged under 13.

_____

_____

_____

2
1
0

(*b*) Tarik Waziz wishes to be added to the list. He is 12 years old, lives in Edinburgh and is interested in wrestling. What must be done to include Tarik in the penfriend list?

_____

_____

1
0

(*c*) Many pupils wish to make contact with a penfriend by email. Suggest how information could be included in the database to indicate those who are able to communicate by email.

_____

_____

_____

[Turn over

KU | PS

5. More and more people are using computers to shop, work from home, contact people from anywhere in the world and gain an education.

(a) Write down **two** advantages for people who work from home rather than in an office.

1 _____

_____

2 _____

2
1
0

_____

(b) Education in the future might not be based in a school but from a computer at your home. Suggest **one** disadvantage of learning from home.

_____

_____

1
0

(c) Give **one** example of a type of job which might require fewer workers as a result of the expanding use of computers. Explain your answer.

_____

_____

1
0

(d) Concern is mounting that some people in society might not be part of this new computer world. Give **one** disadvantage of not being part of this new computer world.

_____

_____

1
0

DO NOT
WRITE IN
THIS MARGIN

KU | PS

6. Louise is a keen computing pupil and is considering a career using computers. She sees several job advertisements from Coverall Insurance for *systems analysts, programmers* and *data preparation operators.*

(a) Describe **two** tasks associated with each job.

Systems analyst

1 _____

2 _____

Programmer

1 _____

2 _____

Data preparation operator

1 _____

2 _____

6
5
4
3
2
1
0

(b) The payroll program for Coverall Insurance is done using a *master file* and a *transaction file*. Both of these files contain a unique employee ID number to identify each worker. The following records are taken from the two files.

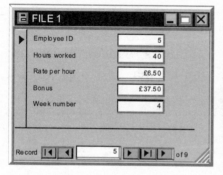

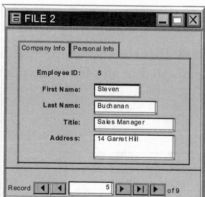

(i) State whether each file is a master file or a transaction file.

FILE 1 _____

FILE 2 _____

2
1
0

[Turn over

KU	PS

6. (b) (continued)

(ii) The payroll task is carried out once a week. What type of processing would be used for the payroll task?

_____

(margin: 1 0)

(c) (i) Many companies are concerned about the costs associated with computers. Apart from the initial cost of buying the computers, explain **one** other cost which would cause concern to the company.

_____

_____

(margin: 1 0)

(ii) Describe **one** possible saving for the company from using computers.

_____

_____

(margin: 1 0)

(d) When information is given to the company by customers, the company must try to ensure that the data is correctly input. Describe **one** way in which this might be done.

_____

_____

(margin: 2 1 0)

(e) Do you think that the increasing use of computers reduces the amount of paper generated in an office? Explain your answer.

_____

_____

_____

(margin: 2 1 0)

(f) Coverall stores some information on *microfiche*.

  (i) Describe this method of output.

_____

_____

_____

  (ii) Write down **one** disadvantage of using this type of output.

_____

_____

[Turn over for Question 7 on *Page sixteen*

7. The LearnIT Driving School uses a simulator to train new car drivers for the first few lessons.

(a) Suggest **two** reasons for using a simulator to teach people to drive.

1 _____

_____

2 _____

_____

(b) The simulation must operate in *real time*.

(i) Explain what real time means.

_____

_____

(ii) Give **one** example of a problem that would occur if this simulation was not in real time.

_____

_____

(c) The simulator uses a steering wheel connected to the computer as one of its input devices. Does this provide an *analogue* or *digital* signal? Explain your answer.

_____

_____

_____

(d) Suggest **one** output device which might be used by the simulator and describe what it would be used for.

_____

_____

_____

[END OF QUESTION PAPER]

[BLANK PAGE]

C

0560/403

NATIONAL
QUALIFICATIONS
2001

TUESDAY, 5 JUNE
10.35 AM – 12.20 PM

COMPUTING STUDIES
STANDARD GRADE
Credit Level

Read each question carefully.

Attempt **all** questions.

Write your answers in the answer book provided. **Do not** write on the question paper.

Write as neatly as possible.

Answer in sentences wherever possible.

SCOTTISH
QUALIFICATIONS
AUTHORITY

©

	KU	PS

1. Gurmeet is considering selling CDs on the Internet. The Internet is a Wide Area Network available all over the world.

(a) He has a computer system and a printer. What other **two** items would he need to gain access to the Internet? **2**

(b) Gurmeet only uses his computer to play games. To help him run a business using the computer, he knows he must purchase an *integrated package* or separate *application packages*.

   (i) Give **two** advantages of an integrated package. **2**

   (ii) Give **two** disadvantages of an integrated package. **2**

(c) One of Gurmeet's employees has poor eyesight. Describe **two** ways in which her **computer system** could be adapted to make it easier for her to use the computer. **2**

(d) Gurmeet decides to buy an integrated package. He wants to use a database to keep details of customers.

   (i) What legislation covers storage of other peoples' personal details on a computer? **1**

   (ii) State who is the *data user* (also known as the data controller) in this example. **1**

(e) Gurmeet wishes to use the database part of the integrated package to keep the following details of customers and their purchases.

Title	Initials	Surname
Street	Town	Country
Postcode	Bank details	
Dates of purchases	Price of purchases	Total spent to date

Each customer record would be a maximum of 500 bytes. His floppy discs hold 1·44 megabytes. How many customer records could be held on one floppy disc? **Show all working**. **3**

(f) Gurmeet wishes to produce a list of sales for each town in the UK. The list should display the **Towns** in alphabetic order and **Total spent to date** should be from most spent to least spent. Describe the steps necessary to produce this list. **4**

KU | PS

2. An administration assistant at a school uses a spreadsheet to calculate what departments spend on computer supplies and books.

Part of the spreadsheet is shown below.

	A	B	C	D	E	F
1		Computer Supplies	Books	Total	Discount	Final Cost
2	**Department**					
3	Art	4·62	200·30	204·92		20·49	184·43
4	Computing	88·31	200·04	288·35		
5	Technological Studies	68·25	150·00	218·25		
6	Business Studies	56·19	160·21	216·40		
7	English	10·05	210·20	220·25		
8						
9	**Discount is**	**10%**				

(a) Which type of referencing would have been used to copy the formula from D3 to the other cells in that column? | | 1

(b) (i) A discount is given to each department if they spend more than £200. Give a formula for cell E3. | | 4

    (ii) We wish to replicate this formula down column E. Which cell in the formula would require an *absolute reference*? | | 1

(c) How can the administration assistant stop the cell which contains the discount percentage from being altered by accident? | 1

(d) The administration assistant can change the *Human Computer Interface* (HCI) of the spreadsheet package. Suggest **one** possible change. | 1

(e) The *cell attributes* of B3 to F7 are to be altered.

    (i) What is meant by the term cell attributes? | 1

    (ii) Suggest a suitable alteration which could be made. | 1

(f) The school wishes to buy a new software package which requires **32 megabytes** of backing store. The software can be distributed either on floppy discs or CD ROM.

State **one** disadvantage of choosing the floppy discs. | 1

[Turn over

KU | PS

3.

Jodi has heard about a new type of robot cleaner that can vacuum a room unsupervised. Jodi goes to a demonstration of the robot cleaner and is amazed to see the robot cleaner go round objects in its path.

(*a*) (i) Name **two** types of sensor which will allow the robot to be aware of objects.

(ii) Is it likely that the robot cleaner is controlled by an *open loop* or a *closed loop*? Give a reason for your answer.

(*b*) The robot can be fitted with different types of *end effector*.

(i) What is an end effector?

(ii) Give an example of a suitable end effector for this robot.

(*c*) The robot cleaner's programs were written using a *control language* and the programs are stored in *ROM*.

(i) Why are programs written using a control language?

(ii) Give **one** reason for *control software* being stored in ROM.

(*d*) Most programs must be translated before they are implemented. Name one type of *translator*.

KU values: 2, 1, 1
PS values: 2, 1, 1, 1

KU | PS

4. Liam bought a computer that was advertised in the local newspaper.

NEW 2000

32-bit computer
128 megabytes RAM
10 megabytes ROM
900 MHz
25 gigabytes hard disc
Multi-programming OS
Multimedia

(a) What is the *word* length of this computer?

> PS: 1

(b) This computer has 128 megabytes of *RAM*. Explain how a CPU can locate a particular area of memory.

> KU: 1

(c) The operating system of the computer supports *multi-programming*.

(i) Explain the term multi-programming.

> KU: 2

(ii) Give **one** advantage to the **user** of using a computer with multi-programming capabilities.

> PS: 1

(d) The operating system of the computer supports *multimedia*.

Give **one** advantage to the **user** of using a computer with multimedia capabilities.

> PS: 1

(e) Different types of data can be stored in memory.

(i) How is *text* represented in memory?

> KU: 1

(ii) What data representation is used to store very large numbers?

> KU: 1

[Turn over

| | KU | PS |

5. Best Ever Games is a company which supplies computer games to shops throughout Britain.

(a) The box for each game has a bar code. The last digit in the code is a *check digit*.

   (i) What is the purpose of a check digit? — KU 1

   (ii) From what data is the check digit calculated? — KU 1

   (iii) How would an invalid code be identified? — KU 1

(b) The Data Processing Manager has designed an order form which can be read by the computer system using *optical character recognition* (*OCR*).

   (i) Explain the term OCR. — KU 1

   (ii) Give **two** advantages of using OCR. — PS 2

(c) The company makes regular backups. How many generations of *file ancestry* would you recommend should be kept?

Explain your answer. You may use a diagram. — PS 2

(d) The police notify the company that they have caught a group of people writing viruses.

   (i) What legislation covers deliberate spreading of a computer virus? — KU 1

   (ii) Name **one** other illegal activity covered by that legislation. — KU 1

   (iii) Another current piece of legislation is the Copyright, Designs and Patents Act. How does this Act protect the company? — KU 1

(e) A shop, which Best Ever Games supplies games to, uses *interactive processing* to process all customer transactions.

Give **two** benefits to the customer of interactive processing. — PS 2

	KU	PS

6. Flavia is in charge of inviting former pupils to a dinner to celebrate her school's 50th anniversary. Kris, who teaches Computing Studies, suggested that Flavia create a *standard letter* using an integrated package.

(a) (i) What is a standard letter? — KU 2

(ii) The standard letter is stored in one file. Describe the other file required to produce personalised invitations. — PS 1

(b) When Flavia printed out the letter its appearance was different from the appearance of the letter on the screen. Kris said that they must be using the wrong *printer driver*.

(i) What is a printer driver? — KU 1

(ii) What is the purpose of a printer driver? — KU 1

(c) A database file is kept to record ticket sales. A single record from this file is shown below.

RECORD 3

Name	A Fox
Ticket Cost	£6·00
Number Required	4
Total Cost	£24·00
Enrolment Year	1980

(i) What type of field is Total Cost? — KU 1

(ii) How would the computer work out the Total Cost? — PS 2

(d) Flavia creates a spreadsheet to keep a record of ticket sales for every student Enrolment Year. Here is a copy of part of the spreadsheet.

	A	B	C	D
1	**Enrolment Year**	**Tickets sold**		
2	1990	200		
3	1991	350		
4	1992	180		

(i) Explain how Flavia could use this data to produce a chart. — PS 2

(ii) What type of data linkage would allow the chart to update automatically as new ticket sales figures were entered? — KU 1

(e) Flavia wishes to produce a magazine for the anniversary.

Which facility of the package would be used to place the school name at the top of the page? — KU 1

[END OF QUESTION PAPER]

[BLANK PAGE]

[BLANK PAGE]

FOR OFFICIAL USE

G

KU   PS

Total Marks

0560/402

NATIONAL
QUALIFICATIONS
2002

FRIDAY, 31 MAY
G/C 1.00 PM – 2.15 PM
F/G 2.20 PM – 3.35 PM

COMPUTING STUDIES
STANDARD GRADE
General Level

Fill in these boxes and read what is printed below.

Full name of centre

Town

Forename(s)

Surname

Date of birth
Day Month Year

Scottish candidate number

Number of seat

Read each question carefully.

Attempt **all** questions.

Write your answers in the space provided on the question paper.

Write as neatly as possible.

Answer in sentences wherever possible.

Before leaving the examination room you must give this book to the invigilator. If you do not, you may lose all the marks for this paper.

SCOTTISH
QUALIFICATIONS
AUTHORITY

1. Sam works for the local radio station in Maintown. One of Sam's jobs is to type radio scripts using word processing software.

Sam shows the finished script to the producer. The producer asks Sam to change the script so that paragraph 5 comes before paragraph 4.

(a) (i) What feature of the word processing software can Sam use to make this change without typing either of the paragraphs again?

_____

(ii) Describe clearly the steps involved in using this feature to move paragraph 5 so it is before paragraph 4.

_____

_____

_____

(b) (i) Sam has typed a script for a radio interview. One of the people involved, Mr McNeish, is unable to take part in the interview because he is ill. Mr Brown has offered to do the interview instead.

What feature of the word processing software can Sam use to alter all occurrences of "Mr McNeish" to "Mr Brown" as quickly as possible?

_____

(ii) Describe clearly how Sam would use this feature to alter the script so that it is correct for Mr Brown.

_____

_____

_____

(c) Many people write to the radio station asking for information. Sam has to reply to many of these letters. Sam uses *standard paragraphs* for this task.

What is meant by a standard paragraph?

_____

_____

1. (continued)

(*d*) Give **two** reasons why using standard paragraphs will increase Sam's productivity for this task.

1 _____

_____

2 _____

_____

2
1
0

(*e*) Some of the radio programmes produced by the station must be kept secret until they are broadcast. This is because other radio stations or newspapers could be interested in the stories they contain.

Give **two** ways that the radio station can stop people getting access to the files stored on Sam's computer.

1 _____

_____

2 _____

_____

2
1
0

(*f*) The *initial* cost for all the hardware and software needed for Sam's computer system was over two thousand pounds, but Sam still finds that there are a number of *running* costs for the system.

Give **one** possible running cost for Sam's computer system.

_____

_____

1
0

[Turn over

2. Chris is manager of an outdoor activities centre in Glen Osprey. Chris uses a spreadsheet to store details of the number of people taking part in each activity. Here is an example of one of the spreadsheets.

	A	B	C	D	E
1	Activity	Time (hours)	Group size	Cost per person	Group activity cost
2	sailing	1.5	40	£5.00	£200.00
3	climbing	2.5	42	£4.29	£180.18
4	white water rafting	1	21	£7.16	£150.36
5	canoeing	2	16	£4.20	£67.20
6				Total	£597.74
7					

Chris alters group size for sailing to 45 and the figures displayed in cells E2 and E6 change straight away.

(a) (i) What formula has been entered in cell E2?

_____

(ii) What formula has been entered in cell E6?

_____

(b) When Chris created the spreadsheet, the contents of cells E3, E4 and E5 were not typed separately.

What feature of the spreadsheet was used to create the contents of these cells, based upon the contents of cell E2?

_____

(c) Chris has been asked to include orienteering as an extra activity. Explain what Chris will have to do to **make room** for this new activity in the spreadsheet shown above.

_____

_____

KU PS

2
1
0

2
1
0

1
0

2
1
0

	KU	PS

2. (continued)

(d) When Chris first entered the spreadsheet data, the text "white water rafting" did not fit properly into cell A4 as shown below.

	A	B
1	Activity	Time (hours)
2	sailing	1.5
3	climbing	2.5
4	white water ra	1
5	canoeing	2

What did Chris do so that the full name of the activity "white water rafting" appeared properly in cell A4?

_____

_____

1
0

(e) When Chris first created the spreadsheet, the data in column E appeared as shown below.

E
Group activity cost
200
180.18
150.36
67.2
597.74

Explain clearly how Chris was able to make the costs display as money.

_____

_____

_____

2
1
0

[Turn over

2. (continued)

(f) Chris has to produce reports for the owner of the centre. These reports include written information as well as figures or charts taken from spreadsheets.

Give **two** reasons why Chris prefers to use an *integrated package* to do this task.

1 _____

2 _____

2
1
0

(g) Jo is the assistant manager at the centre. Chris wants Jo to be able to use the spreadsheet package properly. Jo has never used a spreadsheet before.

(i) Should Jo use the *on-line help* or *on-line tutorial* to get started?

_____

1
0

(ii) Explain your answer.

_____

_____

_____

1
0

3. Lesley works at the local garden centre. People often ask questions about the best type of plants to buy. Lesley has made a database to help answer these questions. Here are two **records** from the database.

Plant Name	Daffodil
Colour(s) of flower	Yellow, Orange
Height (metres)	0.3
Flowering months(s)	March, April
Price (each)	£0.24

Plant Name	Rhododendron
Colour(s) of flower	Purple, Pink
Height (metres)	2.1
Flowering months(s)	April, May
Price (each)	£16.90

(a) A customer is looking for tall plants to provide shade in a large garden. Explain clearly how Lesley could obtain a list on the screen of the tallest plants available, starting with the largest one.

_____

_____

_____

3
2
1
0

(b) A customer would like a list of plants which will have purple flowers in April. Explain clearly how Lesley would obtain this list.

_____

_____

_____

3
2
1
0

[Turn over

3. (continued)

(c) Lesley decides to make the database available to customers to allow them to answer some of their own questions in the shop. Lesley decides **not** to use a mouse and GUI (graphical user interface), as some people may not know how to use a mouse. Lesley can alter the software's user interface to get **either** a *command driven* package or a *menu driven* package.

(i) Which interface should Lesley choose for beginners to use?

_____

(ii) Explain your answer.

_____

_____

_____

Lesley makes a poster to advertise the database system as she already has some photographs of plants.

(d) What input device will Lesley need to include these photographs in the poster?

_____

(e) Lesley places an image in the middle of the page but it is too large. Name a feature of a graphics package that can make it the correct size.

_____

4. Punctual Parcels collect and deliver parcels all over Scotland. Parcels must be taken to a local office of Punctual Parcels to begin their journey. The company aims to deliver all parcels the next day. Whenever Punctual Parcels accept a parcel at one of its offices, a form has to be filled in by the customer, and the time the parcel was handed over is recorded.

Parcel from	Parcel to
Name:	Name:
Address:	Address:
Postcode:	Postcode:
Office use only	Parcel Number:
Date received:	Time received:
Weight:	Cost:

The details are entered into a microcomputer at the local office. All the computers are linked to the mainframe computer at the company Head Office.

(*a*) What type of network is this?

_____

1
0

(*b*) When the form is being typed, the program carries out various checks on the data being entered. Choose **one** of the fields shown in the form above and explain clearly how the program can check the data.

_____

_____

2
1
0

_____

(*c*) As each form is typed, the microcomputer transmits it to the mainframe computer. A unique Parcel Number is sent straight back to the office to be written on the parcel label. What type of processing is being used here?

_____

1
0

[Turn over

KU | PS

4.   (continued)

(d) The last digit of the Parcel Number is a *check digit*. Explain clearly what is meant by a check digit.

_____

_____

2
1
0

(e) (i) Each night the **parcels** are sorted by postcodes and transported in vans to the local delivery offices. When the parcel is delivered the next day, the delivery person fills in the time on a form, and collects a signature as shown below.

Parcel No	Address	Time Delivered	Signature
345678	3 Main Street, Drumlochty	1.45pm	John Jones
346123	7 Burns Place, Drumlochty	1.54pm	M.Thomson
346139	7 Burns Place, Drumlochty	1.54pm	M.Thomson
345433	18 Burns Place Drumlochty	2.08pm	S.Dunbar

At the end of the day, the data from these forms is also entered into the computer system as a data file. This data file is then processed overnight to **update** the data stored on record from the original form. What type of processing is this?

_____

1
0

(ii) On which field will the records in the data file be sorted before updating takes place?

_____

1
0

(f) (i) Punctual Parcels need a signature when each parcel is delivered. They have decided to test a new system of gathering signatures. Each delivery person is given a small computer system.

What type of computer system is this?

_____

1
0

(ii) How can the customer enter their signature with the new system?

_____

1
0

5. (*a*) Real Panes manufacture double glazing windows. Three years ago, the company decided to automate the production of their double glazing units by introducing robots and CNC machines.

    (i) Give **one disadvantage** to the company of automating the production line.

_____

_____

    (ii) Give **one advantage** to the company of automating the production line.

_____

_____

(*b*) Real Panes were concerned about the safety of workers in the new factory. Give **two** safety precautions they could have used to avoid injury from the robots.

1 _____

2 _____

(*c*) (i) When double glazing units are passed down the production line, each robot only moves when it detects that it has gripped the window unit properly.

    Is this closed loop control or open loop control?

_____

    (ii) Explain your answer.

_____

_____

_____

[Turn over

KU | PS

5. (continued)

(d) At the end of the production line, a light is shone at the window and a sensor behind the glass is moved quickly to cover all parts of the window. The system detects any dirt or damage to the glass by measuring the percentage of light that comes through each part of the window.

(i) Would the sensor used above be analogue or digital?

_____

(ii) Explain your answer.

_____

_____

_____

(e) After each window is manufactured, it is taken to a storage warehouse by a mobile robot. The robot follows exactly the same route to the warehouse each time.

Explain how the robot can follow exactly the same route each time.

_____

_____

6. (*a*) Mhairi works as a programmer for the Nestegg Building Society. Most of Mhairi's programs are written using a *high level language*. State **two** features which are common to all high level languages.

1 _____

_____

2 _____

_____

2
1
0

(*b*) Mhairi has hundreds of files saved on her hard disc. Some of these are *data files* while others are *program files*.

(i) What is meant by a program file?

_____

_____

1
0

(ii) What is the purpose of a data file?

_____

_____

1
0

(*c*) Mhairi loads a program into the main memory of her computer.

(i) What type of main memory will be used?

_____

1
0

(ii) Explain your answer.

_____

_____

1
0

[Turn over

6. **(continued)**

(*d*) A section of memory in Mhairi's computer contains the following whole number values which represent stored text.

storage location 1 --> 72
storage location 2 --> 69
storage location 3 --> 76
storage location 4 --> 76
storage location 5 --> 79

Use the table below to work out what the values mean in these five storage locations.

A	B	C	D	E	F	G	H	I	J	K	L	M	N	O	P	Q	R	S	T
65	66	67	68	69	70	71	72	73	74	75	76	77	78	79	80	81	82	83	84

2
1
0

(*e*) Another section of memory in Mhairi's computer contains the following values, which represent a graphic.

0	0	0	1	0	0	0	0
0	1	1	1	0	0	0	1
0	1	1	1	1	1	1	0
0	0	0	1	1	1	1	0
0	0	0	1	0	0	1	0
0	0	0	0	0	0	0	0

Explain how these values can represent a graphic. You may use the blank grid below to help in your answer.

2
1
0

Page fourteen

KU PS

6. (continued)

(f) Mhairi is having her computer upgraded with a new version of the operating system. State **two** standard features of an operating system.

1 _____

_____

2 _____

_____

2
1
0

(g) As part of the upgrade, Mhairi is going to have the monitor on her desktop computer replaced by a *Liquid Crystal Display* (LCD). The screen area of the new LCD is the same as the monitor it replaces.

Give **two** reasons why Mhairi's company may have decided to change to LCD technology.

1 _____

_____

2 _____

_____

2
1
0

(h) Mhairi finds that her hands are very sore from typing. The doctor says that Mhairi has repetitive strain injury and must completely rest her hands for two months.

(i) What other input method could Mhairi use to continue to enter programs without using her hands?

_____

1
0

(ii) Give **one** possible disadvantage of this method compared to typing for Mhairi.

_____

_____

_____

1
0

[END OF QUESTION PAPER]

[BLANK PAGE]

2002 | Credit

[BLANK PAGE]

C

0560/403

NATIONAL
QUALIFICATIONS
2002

FRIDAY, 31 MAY
2.35 PM – 4.20 PM

COMPUTING STUDIES
STANDARD GRADE
Credit Level

Read each question carefully.

Attempt **all** questions.

Write your answers in the answer book provided. **Do not** write on the question paper.

Write as neatly as possible.

Answer in sentences wherever possible.

SCOTTISH
QUALIFICATIONS
AUTHORITY

	KU	PS

1. A database is kept of all the racehorses in Britain. Details of the horses and their owners are stored. The format of the database is given below.

Field	Sample Data	Field Size (bytes)
Horse's Name:	Firkin's Flyer	15
Age:	4	1
Colour:	Chestnut	8
Height (in hands):	16	1
Owner's Name:	J MacKenzie	30
Owner's Tel No:	01376 269467	13
Owner's Address:	62, Green Street Altonbourgh	60

(a) A black horse, over 15 hands high has been seen running loose. The database is to be used to see whose horse it could be. Explain how the database can be used to do this.

3 (PS)

(b) A new layout is created using the fields shown below. How has the **order** of the list been achieved?

2 (PS)

Horse's Name	Age	Height
Desert Flower	5	18
Red Gin	7	18
Yellow Peril	6	18
Bagshot Brown	4	17
Canterbury Tale	3	17

(c) (i) What is the maximum number of bytes required to store one record of the database?

1 (PS)

(ii) Using your answer from part (i), calculate how many records could be stored on a 1·44 Mb floppy disc. **Show all of your working.**

3 (PS)

(iii) The file has to be edited regularly throughout the day. State the type of access to the file that is required.

1 (PS)

(d) It is necessary to comply with the Data Protection Act of 1998 as personal data is held on the database.

(i) Give **two** requirements of the Data Protection Act that must be complied with.

2 (KU)

(ii) Give **two** rights that the data subjects have under this legislation.

2 (KU)

KU | PS

2. A shop uses a spreadsheet to keep control of its stock as shown below.

	A	B	C	D	E
1	**Item Code**	**Item**	**Current Stock**	**Reorder Level**	**Order**
2	41623	Jumper	12	7	N
3	41634	Shirt	13	15	Y
4	41645	Socks	36	18	N
5	41656	Jacket	4	6	Y

(a) (i) Column E uses a formula that compares the values in column C and column D and places a "Y" or an "N" in column E to show if the item needs to be reordered. What kind of formula would be used in column E?

1

(ii) The formula in cell **E2** was replicated into cells **E3** to **E5**. Would *absolute references* or *relative references* be used in this situation? Give a reason for your answer.

2

(iii) What would be done to stop the formulae in column E from being altered unintentionally?

1

(b) The Item Code in column **A** includes a *check digit*.

(i) Is a check digit an example of *validation* or *verification*?

1

(ii) What is the difference between *validation* and *verification*?

1

(c) The shop buys a new printer. The printer requires a special piece of software.

(i) Name the piece of software.

1

(ii) Why is the piece of software required?

1

(d) An integrated package is used to produce the report on stock levels every month. The table shown above is included in the word processed report. Should *static* or *dynamic data linkage* be used in this case? Justify your answer.

2

(e) The integrated package has a *user-friendly HCI*. Describe **two** features of an HCI that would make it user-friendly.

2

[Turn over

KU | PS

3. The following advert appeared in a computing magazine.

Sense 800 Multimedia PC

- 800 Mhz Processor
- 40 Gb Hard Disc
- 128 SD RAM Memory
- CD ROM/DVD Combined drive
- 3½" Floppy disc drive
- 17" Monitor
- 32 Mb Graphics Card
- 128 Mb 3D Soundcard
- Standard operating system

(a) What is meant by the term *multimedia*?   **1**

(b) One task of the operating system is to manage main memory.

    (i) How does the operating system locate items in main memory?   **2**

    (ii) Name the method used to represent very large numbers stored in main memory.   **1**

    (iii) Explain this method of data representation.   **2**

(c) Mary decides to buy the computer as advertised above and also a scanner. State **two** functions of an operating system which are called upon when scanning an image and storing it on hard disc.   **2**

(d) The Sense 800 also has a *word* size of 128 bits. Mary does not understand what this means. How would you explain it to her?   **2**

(e) Mary also requires some general purpose application software for the computer. She is not sure whether to buy an *integrated package* or several individual *general purpose packages*. Give **two** reasons why she should choose an integrated package.   **2**

	KU	PS

4. Inverdee Airport is considering automating the clearing of snow and ice from its runways.

(a) Before the introduction of any automated system, what should be carried out? **1**

The airport eventually invests in robotic snowploughs to clear the runways.

(b) Name and describe **one** method by which the snowploughs can be taught the route around the airport. **2**

(c) The control programs for the robots are stored on *ROM chips*. Although this is the most expensive way of storing the programs, give **two** reasons why this storage medium is used. **2**

(d) The robots are programmed to blow warm air onto the runways if the temperature is below freezing. Sensors are fitted to the robot so that the computer can activate the blowers automatically.

   (i) This is an example of a *closed loop* system. Why should a closed loop system be used in this case? **1**

   (ii) The temperature constantly varies. What must happen to the data from the sensor so that the computer can process it? **1**

(e) Give **two** arguments that the airport management could use to justify the expense of introducing this system. **2**

[Turn over

	KU	PS

5. A ticket agency has outlets in all of the major towns in Scotland. They sell tickets for hundreds of pop and rock concerts held all over the country. Each outlet has a *remote terminal* connected to a central computer at the company's head office in Glasgow. The central computer holds information about the concerts and the customers who have bought tickets. The company can sell thousands of tickets each day.

(a) What is a remote terminal?

                      KU 1

(b) Suggest a suitable *backing storage medium* for holding the data. Give **one** reason for your answer.

                      PS 2

(c) The central computer allows *multi-access*.

  (i) Explain what is meant by the term "multi-access".

                      KU 2

  (ii) Why is a multi-access system required in this case?

                      PS 1

(d) At the end of each day a back-up copy is made of the database. Three generations of back-up are kept. Describe this back-up process.

                      KU 3

(e) The tickets are printed at the remote terminal when they are purchased. Give **one** reason for using *preprinted stationery* in this case.

                      PS 1

(f) A concert has been postponed and letters need to be sent to all of the people who have bought tickets.

  (i) *Standard letters* are produced to send to all of the people. What is a standard letter?

                      KU 1

  (ii) What is the name given to the process of using a computer to insert all of the personal details from the database into the standard letters in a single operation?

                      KU 1

  (iii) These letters are produced on a laser printer. There are several kinds of printers available which could print the tickets. Give a reason why the ticket agency might choose a laser printer to carry out this task.

                      PS 1

	KU	PS

6. Lachlan writes programs for a computer games company called Webbsoft Leisure. They write their programs using a *high level language* because it is *portable*.

(a) What is meant by the term "portable"? — KU **1**

(b) High level language programs need to be translated so that the computer can understand them. The three types of translator are *assembler*, *compiler* and *interpreter*.

  (i) Why is an assembler unsuitable for this company? — PS **1**

  (ii) Lachlan decides to use an interpreter. Give **one** reason why this may be a good choice and **one** reason why it may be inappropriate. — PS **2**

(c) Lachlan has poor eyesight. Describe **two** ways in which he can change the parameters of the HCI so that it is easier for him to see what is on the screen. — PS **2**

(d) Webbsoft Leisure are concerned that "hackers" are gaining unauthorised access to the company network to see the games that are being developed. Which legislation outlaws this activity? — KU **1**

(e) Webbsoft Leisure holds all company files on a local area network.

  (i) Describe **three** advantages of using a local area network. — KU **3**

  (ii) Access to employee data is restricted to the personnel department. How can this be managed on the network? — PS **2**

[END OF QUESTION PAPER]

[BLANK PAGE]

[BLANK PAGE]

FOR OFFICIAL USE

G

KU   PS

Total Marks

0560/402

NATIONAL
QUALIFICATIONS
2003

THURSDAY, 22 MAY
10.20 AM – 11.35 AM

COMPUTING STUDIES
STANDARD GRADE
General Level

Fill in these boxes and read what is printed below.

Full name of centre

Town

Forename(s)

Surname

Date of birth
Day Month Year

Scottish candidate number

Number of seat

Read each question carefully.

Attempt **all** questions.

Write your answers in the space provided on the question paper.

Write as neatly as possible.

Answer in sentences wherever possible.

Before leaving the examination room you must give this book to the invigilator. If you do not, you may lose all the marks for this paper.

SCOTTISH
QUALIFICATIONS
AUTHORITY

©

1. Hanan runs a business to organise parties for people. She is responsible for organising the invitations, the location and food.

   Hanan helps customers to choose some of the wording for their invitations from a collection of *standard paragraphs*.

   (a) What is meant by a "standard paragraph"?

   _____

   _____

   Hanan has typed out the invitation for a children's party. She has typed "Cocoa the Clown" several times in the invitation, then realises that it should be "Coco the Clown".

   (b) It is possible to change "Cocoa" to "Coco" throughout the invitation in one operation.

   (i) Name the feature which would enable her to do this.

   _____

   (ii) Describe how Hanan would use this feature in this example.

   _____

   _____

   (c) When Hanan first started her business, each invitation was produced on a typewriter.

   Give **one** reason why Hanan prefers to use a word processing package.

   _____

   _____

1. (continued)

Hanan uses the spell check feature in her word processing program to look for mistakes in the invitations.

Here are three lines from an invitation which Hanan has to spell check.

> Miss MacKay requests the pleasure of your company
> as she celebrates her 25th birthday on Saturday
> 18th June 2003. She hops to see you there.

(d) In line 1, the spell check queries a word spelled correctly. Which word does it query and why did the program suggest a possible error here?

_____

_____

_____

_____

2
1
0

(e) In line 3, the word "hops" should have been written as "hopes". Why did the spelling check not find the error?

_____

_____

_____

_____

1
0

(f) Hanan is writing a five page report about her business. She makes a hard copy of the full report. She then makes changes to the last three pages. How can Hanan print out only the pages which have changed?

_____

_____

_____

2
1
0

[Turn over

2. Passable Patios are a company which designs and installs patios. Les works as a salesperson for Passable Patios.

When Les visits a house, he measures the area for the patio and helps the owners choose a building material.

Les uses a computer to calculate the cost during the visit to the house.

(a) (i) Suggest a suitable type of computer for this task.

_____

(ii) Give a reason for your answer.

_____

_____

Here is an example of the basic spreadsheet which Les uses to get estimates for customers.

	A	B	C	D	E
1	Passable Patios - Estimate				
2					
3	Item	Unit Cost	Quantity required	Item Cost	
4	Grey monoblock	0.2	500	100	
5	Red monoblock	0.26	130	33.8	
6	Foundation (bag)	1.81	16	28.96	
7	Labour (hours)	8	32	256	
8			Total	418.76	
9					

(b) The contents of cell D4 have been calculated by the computer. Suggest a formula that could have been entered in cell D4.

_____

(c) The contents of cell D8 have also been calculated by the computer. Suggest a formula that could have been entered in cell D8.

_____

2. **(continued)**

(d) When Les made the original spreadsheet, he did not have to type all the formulas. He was able to *replicate* some of them.

(i) Which cell contained the formula to be replicated?

_____

(ii) Which cells did it need to be replicated into?

_____

(e) The customer decides also to include some black monoblock bricks. Explain what Les will have to do to the spreadsheet **before** he enters the data.

_____

_____

(f) Les wants all the costs in column D to appear as money. Explain how Les will do this.

_____

_____

(g) When Les bought his computer the salesperson recommended that he should buy a full spreadsheet package rather than an integrated package containing a spreadsheet.

(i) Give **one** reason why Les might prefer the full spreadsheet package.

_____

_____

(ii) Give **one** reason why Les might prefer the integrated package.

_____

_____

[Turn over

3. The LochenMhor Tourist Information Centre provides information for visitors.

Visitors can be placed on the mailing list so that they can get up-to-date information about events. The Tourist Information Centre keeps this information on a computerised database. Here is an example of one record from the database.

Title	Miss
Initial	R
Last Name	Smith
Interests	Hill-walking, Sailing, Golfing
Months Visiting	June, July
Address	100 Main Street Binhexeter Suffolk

Martyn works at the Tourist Information Centre. He thinks it would be a good idea to get a printed copy of the whole mailing list.

He decides to get the list printed in order of the people's names.

(a) Describe how Martyn can use the database package to get the list in the right order.

_____

_____

2
1
0

(b) A fishing competition has been organised for June. Describe how Martyn can use the database to obtain the records of people who might be interested in this event.

_____

_____

_____

3
2
1
0

3. (continued)

Some people have expressed concerns about the security of their personal details.

(c) Describe **two** methods that Martyn could use to keep the data secure.

1 _____

_____

2 _____

_____

2
1
0

(d) The law requires that Martyn must do various things to safeguard the data about individuals stored on the system.

(i) Name the Act which applies here.

_____

1
0

(ii) As well as keeping the data secure, give **two** things that Martyn must do to comply with this law.

1 _____

_____

2 _____

_____

2
1
0

(e) Martyn's computer has various *running costs*. Describe **two** of these running costs.

1 _____

_____

2 _____

_____

2
1
0

[Turn over

4. Sionead is the manager of a furniture superstore in Inverness.

The computer which handles all of the orders is sited in Edinburgh at the company headquarters. Terminals in each branch are connected to this computer by telephone lines.

(*a*) What type of network is this?

_____

(*b*) The company uses a *mainframe* computer to do its processing. Give **two** reasons why a mainframe computer is suited to this task.

1 _____

2 _____

When a customer wants to buy a product, the details, including the customer's ID number, are first written on a paper form then typed into a computer system.

(*c*) Each customer ID number includes a *check digit*. What is a check digit and why is it used?

_____

_____

(*d*) Each night the central computer works out the total orders for each type of furniture from the orders placed at all of the branches that day.

(i) Is this *interactive* processing or *batch* processing?

_____

(ii) Explain your answer.

_____

_____

4. (continued)

The superstore sends a bill to customers each month. The customer tears off the bottom section of the bill, fills in the amount they want to pay, and sends this bottom section back to the superstore with their payment.

The customer details are **already filled in** on this bottom section of the bill, ready to be input to the computer system when it is sent back.

(*e*) What do you call a document where the computer has already filled in some of the details when printing the bill? Complete the missing word.

T_____ Document

(*f*) To set up and make this system work properly, the following people were required.

> *systems analyst*
> *computer operator*
> *data preparation operator*

Choose **any two** of these jobs and write them in the boxes provided. Below each box, clearly describe **one** task which that job involves.

(i) | Job |

Description _____

_____

_____

(ii) | Job |

Description _____

_____

_____

[Turn over

KU | PS

5. Ashraf works for a company which organises firework displays. He decides to visit his supplier's factory to find out about the latest fireworks.

Ashraf finds that the factory has been automated. Robots are now used to manufacture fireworks and transport materials.

(a) Suggest **two** safety precautions which could have been used in the factory to avoid injury to the workers from the robots.

1 _____

_____

2 _____

_____

**2
1
0**

(b) As each firework is manufactured, the exact quantity of each ingredient is measured by weighing it using computer control.

(i) Is this an example of *open loop control* or *closed loop control*?

_____

**1
0**

(ii) Explain your answer.

_____

_____

_____

**1
0**

(c) Ashraf speaks to one of the workers who worked in the factory before it was automated. Suggest **two** ways in which the worker's job may have changed since the factory was automated.

1 _____

_____

2 _____

_____

**2
1
0**

KU | PS

5. (continued)

(*d*) The manager of the factory shows Ashraf a computer program which provides a simulation of a firework display. The effect of each of the factory's different fireworks can be viewed using this simulation.

Give **two** reasons why Ashraf would use such a simulation.

1 _____

_____

2 _____

_____

2
1
0

[Turn over

6. Jill runs an Internet café. Visitors to the café pay to access Internet services like e-mail and the World Wide Web.

Jill has chosen to use OXSI as the *operating system* on the computers in the Internet café.

(a) Give **two** standard functions of an operating system.

1 _____

_____

2 _____

_____

2
1
0

(b) Jill can alter the user interface of the computers depending on what each customer requires. There are options to have either a *menu driven system*, a *graphical user interface* or a *command driven interface*.

Jill selects the graphical user interface to make it easier to use for beginners. Give **two** reasons why a graphical user interface is easier for a beginner.

1 _____

_____

2 _____

_____

2
1
0

(c) Jill has had several enquiries from tourists who want to send pictures to friends along with their e-mails.

The tourists have brought the photographs along with them.

What piece of hardware will Jill use to input the photographs?

_____

1
0

6. (continued)

(d) One of the visitors to the Internet café asks Jill about the difference between *data files* and *program files*.

(i) What is a program file?

_____

_____

(ii) What is a data file?

_____

_____

(e) Jill has some systems set up with voice output capability.

(i) Describe a situation where this might be useful for a customer to use.

_____

_____

_____

_____

(ii) What output device is required for voice output?

_____

(f) Jill's regular customers sign a form to get a discount. One customer asks Jill if she could use *handwriting recognition* to store the shape of her signature on a computer. Jill says this is not possible. Give a reason why.

_____

_____

_____

[Turn over

KU PS

1
0

1
0

1
0

1
0

1
0

KU | PS

7. Kenneth works from home as a programmer.

He has recently bought a laser printer. When he uses it, some of the characters do not print correctly. Kenneth thinks that it must be using the wrong *character set*.

(a) Explain clearly what is meant by a "character set".

_____

_____

_____

(b) Kenneth uses a *high level language* to write programs. When he has finished writing a program, he uses a translator program to convert it into machine code.

Explain why the high level language program must be converted into machine code.

_____

_____

_____

_____

(c) (i) While Kenneth is typing a program, is it being stored in *RAM* or *ROM*?

_____

(ii) Explain your answer.

_____

_____

7. (continued)

(d) While Kenneth is working on a program, he will regularly save the program as a file on backing store. His computer system has a *hard disk drive*, a *CD-ROM drive* and a *magnetic tape drive*.

(i) Which drive will Kenneth use to regularly save his program?

_____

(ii) Which drive will Kenneth use to make a *backup* of his program files?

_____

(e) Kenneth is considering buying a new computer system. Compared to his old computer, the new computer will have twice the size of *main memory* and a microprocessor which is twice as fast.

(i) Give **one** advantage to Kenneth of having twice as much main memory.

_____

_____

_____

(ii) Give **one** advantage to Kenneth of having a microprocessor which is twice as fast.

_____

_____

_____

[END OF QUESTION PAPER]

[BLANK PAGE]

[BLANK PAGE]

C

0560/403

NATIONAL QUALIFICATIONS 2003

THURSDAY, 22 MAY 1.00 PM – 2.45 PM

COMPUTING STUDIES
STANDARD GRADE
Credit Level

Read each question carefully.

Attempt **all** questions.

Write your answers in the answer book provided. **Do not** write on the question paper.

Write as neatly as possible.

Answer in sentences wherever possible.

SCOTTISH QUALIFICATIONS AUTHORITY

©

	KU	PS

1. A bank stores customer records on a computerised database. The employees in the bank have access to the database to help them deal with customers. They use a *wide-area network* to connect the bank's offices and branches.

(a) This network is *multi-access*.

    (i) What is meant by the term "multi-access"?   **2**

    (ii) Why is a multi-access system a necessity for the bank?   **1**

(b) The bank employees have usernames and passwords. They are encouraged to change their passwords regularly. *Verification* is carried out when passwords are changed.

    (i) What is the purpose of "verification"?   **1**

    (ii) Explain how this computer system could verify a new password that the user is entering.   **1**

(c) The bank is concerned that unauthorised people could be accessing confidential customer files. This is referred to as *hacking*.

    (i) Which piece of legislation outlaws this?   **1**

    (ii) State another activity that is outlawed by this legislation.   **1**

    (iii) Apart from the use of usernames and passwords, describe **one** other way in which unauthorised access can be stopped.   **1**

(d) Customers need to be served as quickly as possible. All transactions are processed immediately.

    (i) What type of processing is carried out in this situation?   **1**

    (ii) Why is it important to the customers that the bank use this type of processing?   **1**

    (iii) Customer details are stored on hard disk. Their details need to be accessed quickly on an individual basis. Name this type of access.   **1**

KU | PS

1. (continued)

(e) Customers complete application forms for new accounts as shown below.

Bank Account Application Form
(Please complete this form using block capitals)

NAME:

ADDRESS:

POSTCODE: TELEPHONE NUMBER:

ACCOUNT APPLIED FOR:

The information on the forms can be entered into the bank's computer system using *Optical Character Recognition*.

(i) Name the hardware device that is required for Optical Character Recognition.

1

(ii) What is meant by "Optical Character Recognition"?

2

(iii) Why is it necessary for the form to be completed using block capitals?

1

[Turn over

KU | PS

2. A holiday company keeps a database of all of the hotels in Scotland. A record from the database is shown below.

Hotel ID	2365
Hotel Name	The Royal
Address	15, Station Road
Town/City	Glasgow
Postcode	AT89 4ED
Telephone number	01368 927385
No of Rooms	18
Rating (stars)	4
Facilities	Swimming Pool, Games Room

(a) A customer contacts the holiday company asking for a list of the hotels in Edinburgh in descending order of rating. Hotels with the same rating are to be listed in alphabetical order of hotel name. Describe how the database could be used to produce this list.

3

(b) Every year the holiday company contacts all of the hotels on the database to see if any of their details have changed. The letters are all similar, with just the details about each hotel differing. Outline the **three** steps required in the production of these letters so as to minimise the work involved.

3

(c) A word processor and database are part of an *integrated package*.

(i) Give **two disadvantages** of using an integrated package instead of separate *application packages*.

2

(ii) An advantage of integrated software is that it has a common *Human Computer Interface* throughout. Why is this an advantage?

1

(d) The holiday company uses another database to hold information on bookings. A record is shown below.

Customer Name	Mr Garcia
Address	25, Gordon Road
Town/City	Risdale
Postcode	RD32 9GS
Hotel ID	2572
Cost per night	£80
Number of nights	4
Total Cost	£320

This database has a *computed field*.

(i) What is meant by the term "computed field"?

1

(ii) Which field in this database will be a computed field?

1

	KU	PS

3. McAdam Academy has just invested in a new computer network to help with the administration in the school. Every member of staff has access to a computer for recording pupil marks, registrations, writing report cards and communicating with other staff.

(a) The headteacher announces that the new network will greatly improve the flow of information around the school. Suggest **two** reasons to justify this statement.

    PS: 2

(b) Because the school has pupil data on the network, the pupils have certain rights according to the Data Protection Act, 1998. List **two** rights that this legislation provides to pupils.

    KU: 2

(c) The files stored on the network are organised using a *hierarchical filing system*. Give **two** reasons why this is the most appropriate filing system for the school.

    PS: 2

(d) The network is to be used by both experienced and inexperienced users.

  (i) *On-line help* is available. What is on-line help?

    KU: 2

  (ii) Why might experienced users prefer a *command driven HCI*?

    PS: 1

  (iii) Why would inexperienced users prefer a *menu driven HCI*?

    PS: 1

(e) One teacher uses the network to produce a report on new teaching methods. The report includes text, diagrams and a table.

  (i) There are several different types of software that she could use to produce the report. Suggest suitable software for this task, giving a reason for your answer.

    PS: 2

  (ii) The report contains a *footer*. What is a "footer"?

    KU: 2

  (iii) What piece of software is required to ensure that the report prints exactly as it appears on screen?

    KU: 1

(f) All software used on the network came on *CD-ROMs*.

  (i) Give **two** reasons why a CD-ROM is a good distribution medium for computer software.

    PS: 2

  (ii) Give **one** difference and **one** similarity between a CD-ROM and a re-writeable optical disk.

    KU: 2

[Turn over

KU | PS

4. Mahdia keeps a record of her golf scores using a spreadsheet. Part of the spreadsheet is shown below.

	A	B	C	D
1	Golf Record			
2				
3	Handicap:	16		
4				
5	Date	Competition	Gross Score	Net Score
6	12/04/03	Wallace Shield	84	68
7	15/04/03	Spring Medal	79	63
8	28/04/03	Campbell Cup	85	69
9	05/05/03	May Medal	83	67

(Note: Mahdia's Net Score is calculated by subtracting her Handicap from her Gross Score.)

(a) Mahdia has entered a formula into cell D6. This formula is *replicated* from D6 into cells D7 to D9.

   (i) What is meant by the term "replicate"?   1

   (ii) Both *relative* and *absolute* replication are required when replicating the formula in column D. Explain why both types of referencing are required in this situation.   2

(b) Mahdia uses the spreadsheet to create a chart to help analyse her scores. She uses *dynamic data linkage*.

   (i) What is meant by the term "dynamic data linkage"?   2

   (ii) Why is this appropriate in this case?   1

(c) The computer that Mahdia uses has an operating system that is capable of *multi-programming*.

   (i) What is meant by the term "multi-programming"?   2

   (ii) How could multi-programming be useful to her?   1

(d) Her computer has a standard *character set* which includes several *control characters*.

   (i) How are characters represented in the computer?   1

   (ii) What is meant by "control characters"?   1

   (iii) Suggest **two** uses of control characters for Mahdia.   2

	KU	PS

5. A microchip manufacturer is investigating the use of robots to produce its new processor chips. As part of their investigation they construct a *virtual reality* model so that they can get an idea of the new factory layout.

(a) (i) What is "virtual reality"? — KU **2**

(ii) Name a piece of hardware used specifically for virtual reality. — KU **1**

The virtual reality simulation helps the manufacturer to realise that many safety measures need to be taken so that human workers can work safely in the proximity of the robots.

(b) Describe **two** possible safety measures that could be applied in the factory. — PS **2**

(c) The robots are designed with four *degrees of freedom*. What does the term "degrees of freedom" mean? — KU **1**

(d) The robots are programmed using a *high level control language*.

(i) Describe what is meant by a "control language". — KU **1**

(ii) Give **one** reason why a high level language is the most suitable choice for the control language. — PS **1**

(iii) While developing the programs, why might the programmers use an *interpreter* to translate the code into machine code but on completion use a *compiler*? — PS **2**

(e) When producing microchips, the conditions such as humidity and temperature must be closely monitored. Sensors are used to monitor these conditions and the settings of the air-conditioning unit are changed accordingly by a computer system.

Is this an example of an *open loop* or a *closed loop* control system? Give a reason for your answer. — PS **2**

(f) Give **two** reasons why the introduction of robots improves the efficiency of a factory. — KU **2**

[END OF QUESTION PAPER]

[BLANK PAGE]

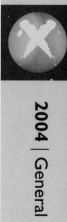

[BLANK PAGE]

FOR OFFICIAL USE

G

	KU	PS
Total Marks		

0560/402

NATIONAL
QUALIFICATIONS
2004

THURSDAY, 13 MAY
10.20 AM – 11.35 AM

**COMPUTING STUDIES
STANDARD GRADE**
General Level

Fill in these boxes and read what is printed below.

Full name of centre

Town

Forename(s)

Surname

Date of birth

Day Month Year   Scottish candidate number   Number of seat

Read each question carefully.

Attempt **all** questions.

Write your answers in the space provided on the question paper.

Write as neatly as possible.

Answer in sentences wherever possible.

Before leaving the examination room you must give this book to the invigilator. If you do not, you may lose all the marks for this paper.

SCOTTISH
QUALIFICATIONS
AUTHORITY

©

KU	PS

1. Kraivie High School would like a poster for pupils telling them about their Activity Day.

First draft

KHS Activity Day

Learning can be fun
Make new friends
Learn a new skill

The first draft looked too plain so a second draft was created.

Second draft

 **KHS Activity Day**

Learning can be fun
Make new friends
Learn a new skill

(*a*) State **two** changes that have been made to the **heading text** in the second draft.

1_____

2_____

**2
1
0**

(*b*) (i) The picture of the school has been scaled. What does the term *scale* mean?

_____

_____

**1
0**

(ii) State **two** other changes which have been made to the graphic.

_____

_____

_____

**2
1
0**

	KU	PS

1. (continued)

(c) The school wishes to put a photograph of pupils on the poster.

Which input device would be needed?

_____

(d) The school has a black and white *laser printer* and a number of *ink jet printers*.

(i) Give **one** advantage of using the laser printer.

_____

_____

(ii) Give **one** disadvantage of using the laser printer.

_____

_____

(e) One of the teachers said that the *running costs* of the ink jet printer were high.

Give an example of a running cost.

_____

(f) The poster was created using a *program file* and a *datafile*.

(i) Explain the term "program file".

_____

_____

(ii) Explain the term "datafile".

_____

_____

[Turn over

2. Kraivie High School sends out individual letters to parents giving details of the activities their child has chosen. On reading through the letter, it is noticed that instead of "Activity Day" the words "Activity Week" have been printed throughout the document.

(a) What feature of the word processing software would allow this mistake to be easily corrected in one operation?

_____

(b) The school used *standard paragraphs* to create these letters. Explain the term "standard paragraph".

_____

_____

(c) When the completed letter was printed it did not fit onto one page. Name **two** changes which would allow the letter to fit onto one page.

1 _____

_____

2 _____

_____

(d) A pupil at the school suggested to the school secretary that she make use of the *on-line tutorial* feature of the package.

Explain the term "on-line tutorial".

_____

_____

_____

DO NOT
WRITE IN
THIS MARGIN

KU | PS

2. (continued)

(e) The school used an integrated package to create the letter.

Give **two** benefits to the user of using an integrated package.

1 _____

_____

2 _____

_____

2
1
0

(f) The school computers operate a *WIMP* style of *HCI*.

(i) What do the letters "HCI" stand for?

H _____ C _____ I _____

1
0

(ii) Why might users like using the WIMP style of HCI?

_____

_____

1
0

(g) A reporter calls at the school to write an article about the Activity Day. He uses a *palmtop computer* to make notes.

(i) Why would the reporter find a palmtop computer useful for this task?

_____

_____

1
0

(ii) The palmtop computer uses an *LCD* screen.

What do the letters "LCD" stand for?

L _____ C _____ D _____

1
0

(iii) A special pen is used instead of a keyboard to input data.

What is the name given to this data input method?

H _____ R _____

1
0

[Turn over

KU | PS

3. Kraivie High School has decided to use the school's computer system to help manage and run the Activity Day Program.

A *datafile* containing some of the details of the Activity Day is shown below.

Forename	Surname	Sex	Year	Event	Transport
Jade	Forbes	F	2	Photography	No
Gavin	Ross	M	1	Football	Yes
Franki	Murphy	F	1	Golf	No
Barry	Miller	M	3	Cinema	Yes
Kiran	Ahmed	F	2	Skating	Yes

(a) The datafile has to be changed to include the cost for each event.

Explain how this could be done.

_____

_____

_____

2
1
0

(b) (i) A list of all activities which need transport is required.

Describe how you could use the database package to obtain this information.

_____

_____

2
1
0

(ii) The list of activities is needed in alphabetic order.

Describe how this could be achieved.

_____

_____

2
1
0

(c) The computers in the school are linked together to form a *local-area network* (LAN).

Give **two** advantages, to the user, of using a LAN.

1 _____

_____

2 _____

_____

2
1
0

3.   (continued)

(*d*) The teachers are concerned that pupils may try to access the Activity Day datafile and alter the activities on offer.

State **two** ways this could be prevented.

1 _____

_____

2 _____

_____

(*e*) All the network users have the choice of saving to a *floppy disk* or a *hard disk* on the network.

(i) Give **one** advantage of saving to floppy disk.

_____

_____

(ii) Give **one** advantage of saving to the hard disk on the network.

_____

_____

[Turn over

4. Kraivie High School has decided to use a spreadsheet to keep track of the Activity Day finances.

The spreadsheet is shown below.

	A	B	C	D	E	F
1	Activity	No of children	Cost per child	Pupils to pay	School to pay	Total Cost to school
2	Cinema	80	6	4.5	1.5	£120.00
3	Football	60	1.5	1	0.5	£30.00
4	Golf	30	3.5	3	0.5	£15.00
5	Photography	20	2.25	2	0.25	£5.00
6	Skating	100	6	4.5	1.5	£150.00
7					TOTAL	£320.00

(a) Some figures are calculated automatically by the use of *formulae.*

   (i) In which cells would each formula appear?

      =B3*E3 would appear in cell _____

      =C3–D3 would appear in cell _____

   (ii) State the formula which would appear in cell F7 _____

(b) A new event of Web Design is to be entered on the spreadsheet.

State the changes which will have to be made to include this activity in the correct place.

_____

_____

_____

(c) Columns C, D and E should have been displayed as money.

Describe the steps needed to make these changes.

1 _____

2 _____

4. **(continued)**

   (*d*) In column A the word "photography" does not fit properly into the cell. How would you solve this problem?

   _____

   _____

                                                    [Turn over

5. Kraivie High School has an account at Cheapest Ever Cash and Carry. The store is visited before Activity Day to purchase snacks for the pupils.

(a) Here is the school's account number | 000136164749 |

(i) Which digit is the check digit?

_____

(ii) What is the purpose of a check digit?

_____

_____

(iii) How is a check digit created?

_____

_____

(b) The shopping can be paid for by cash or *Electronic Funds Transfer* (EFT).

(i) Give **one** advantage to the shopper of paying by EFT.

_____

_____

(ii) Give **one** advantage to the store of the customers using EFT.

_____

_____

(c) The shop assistants key in sales details at a *terminal*.

Explain the term "terminal".

_____

5. **(continued)**

(d) The store stock records are updated at the end of each working day. This is an example of *batch processing*.

Give **two** advantages to the store of using batch processing.

1 _____

_____

2 _____

_____

(e) A *transaction file* is used to update the *master file*.

(i) What is a "transaction file"?

_____

_____

(ii) Give an example of data which may be held in the store's transaction file.

_____

_____

(f) The manager of the store has introduced a *voice recognition system* to restrict access to the main office.

Give **one** advantage and **one** disadvantage to the store of introducing this system.

Advantage

_____

Disadvantage

_____

[Turn over

KU | PS

6. At the skating rink on Kraivie High School's Activity Day, the pupils watched the Automated Rink Sweeper travel at speed round the rink, cleaning the ice.

(a) Give **two** safety precautions that could be taken to ensure that no skater was hit by the Sweeper.

1 _____

2 _____

2
1
0

(b) (i) The Sweeper uses *real-time processing*.

Explain the term "real-time".

_____

_____

1
0

(ii) Name another type of processing.

_____

1
0

(c) The Sweeper has been programmed using a *high level language*.

(i) Give **two** advantages of using a high level language.

1 _____

_____

2 _____

_____

2
1
0

(ii) Part of the ice rink has to be blocked off and the Sweeper will not be allowed to access this area.

What will have to be done to the **computer** controlling the Sweeper?

_____

1
0

KU PS

6. (continued)

(d) (i) The Sweeper's *sensors* send *feedback* to the computer.

Explain the following terms.

Sensor _____

_____

10

Feedback _____

_____

10

(ii) Is the Sweeper an example of an *open loop* system or a *closed loop* system?

_____

10

(e) The computer controlling the Sweeper is running under an *operating system*.

State **two** tasks an operating system would carry out.

1 _____

2 _____

210

(f) Give **two** advantages to the management of using an Automated Sweeper.

1 _____

_____

2 _____

_____

210

[END OF QUESTION PAPER]

[BLANK PAGE]

[BLANK PAGE]

C

0560/403

NATIONAL QUALIFICATIONS 2004

THURSDAY, 13 MAY 1.00 PM – 2.45 PM

COMPUTING STUDIES STANDARD GRADE Credit Level

Read each question carefully.

Attempt **all** questions.

Write your answers in the answer book provided. **Do not** write on the question paper.

Write as neatly as possible.

Answer in sentences wherever possible.

SCOTTISH QUALIFICATIONS AUTHORITY

©

	KU	PS

1. Iona is a secretary for a software development company. She sends out many *standard letters* to customers.

(a) (i) What is a standard letter? — KU 2

   (ii) What is the name of the process in which information from a *datafile* is inserted into the standard letter? — KU 1

(b) A record from the customer datafile is shown below.

Field Name	Sample Data	Field Size
Name	Chang, Alistair	40
Address	26, Station Road	80
Town	Westbury	20
Postcode	WY34 2NH	8
Age	24	2

   (i) How much memory does a single record from the database need? — PS 1

   (ii) How many records from the database could you fit onto a floppy disk that holds 1·44 Mb? — PS 3

(c) (i) Name the legislation that protects the rights of the customers whose details are held in the database. — KU 1

   (ii) Describe **two** rights that this legislation gives the customers. — KU 2

(d) Before printing the letters, Iona always *spell checks* them. Describe in detail how a spell checker works. — KU 2

(e) Name the piece of software that is required to ensure that the printout is the same as it appears on screen. — KU 1

	KU	PS

2. Many buildings have air conditioning systems installed to control the temperature. The system warms up or cools down the building as necessary using heaters and fans.

(a) (i) What device is required to provide *feedback* of the temperature to the system? — PS 1

(ii) Is this system an example of an *open loop* or *closed loop* system? — PS 1

(iii) What type of processing is required for this system? — PS 1

(iv) The temperature can vary continuously. What must be done to the temperature readings so that they are in a form that the computer can process? — PS 1

(b) The software used to control this system is held on a *ROM chip*.

(i) Give **two** advantages of holding the software on a ROM chip. — KU 2

(ii) Give **one** disadvantage of holding the software on a ROM chip. — KU 1

(c) The software is written using a *control language*. Give **one** reason why this is the most suitable language. — PS 1

(d) Give **one** advantage of using a computerised system rather than a manual system. — KU 1

[Turn over

KU | PS

3. Tanya uses a spreadsheet to keep track of her fantasy football team. A section of the spreadsheet is shown below.

	A	B	C	D	E	F
1	Position	Player ID	Player Name	Player Cost (£m)	Week 1 Score	Week 2 Score
2	Goalkeeper	113	J Davidson	3.3	−2	1
3	Defender	202	H Hart	4.4	6	2
4	Defender	209	F Janario	4.1	6	2
5	Defender	273	J McTavish	3.0	0	9
6	Defender	298	B Parnevik	2.8	1	4
7	Midfielder	407	F Leconte	5.1	3	3
8	Midfielder	445	M Daniel	4.7	1	0
9	Midfielder	501	C Michaels	4.5	6	0
10	Forward	601	H Thierry	8.0	7	3
11	Forward	621	J Foe	5.6	3	2
12	Forward	247	D Christian	4.4	6	6
13						
14			TOTALS	49.9	37	32
15	Funds available (£m)	50				
16	Valid team?	YES				

(a) Formulae are used to calculate the column totals in cells **D14**, **E14** and **F14**. The formula in cell **D14** was *replicated* into the other two cells.

   (i) What is meant by the term "replicate"?

1

   (ii) When the formula was replicated, was *relative referencing* or *absolute referencing* used? Explain your answer.

2

(b) Cell **B16** contains a formula to show if a team is valid or not. A team is valid if the total player cost in **D14** is less than or equal to the funds available in **B15**. If a team is valid, the cell shows "YES" and if not, the cell shows "NO". Part of the formula used is given below. What should be entered into the spaces marked A and B?

= _____ (_____ , "YES", "NO")
     ↑   ↑
     A   B

2

	KU	PS

3. (continued)

(c) Tanya uses the chart feature of her spreadsheet software to display her weekly scores. When data is added to the spreadsheet, the chart is updated automatically. What type of *data linkage* is this? — KU 1

(d) Competitors in the fantasy league have the choice of registering their fantasy team by post or on the league's website.

  (i) Name **one** piece of computer hardware and **one** piece of software that Tanya requires to make use of the Internet. — KU 2

  (ii) The Internet site is *multi-access*. What is meant by this term? — KU 2

  (iii) Give **two** reasons why Tanya prefers to use the Internet rather than the post to register her team. — PS 2

[Turn over

	KU	PS

4. Safeprice Superstores is a chain of supermarkets that have stores all over Scotland.

Each store has a central computer with a database that holds details on all of the products that it sells. An example of a record from the database is shown below.

Product ID	002315
Product Manufacturer	Gimballs
Product Name	Chicken Soup
Product Price	£0·57
Stock Level	246
Reorder Level	150
Reorder?	N
Total Value of Stock	£140·22

(a) When a product is purchased, the *barcode* on the product is scanned and the information on the barcode is used to locate the product in the database.

   (i) How is the reading of a barcode validated?   **1**

   (ii) Which field in the database is **always** updated when a product has been purchased?   **1**

   (iii) Should this database be stored on backing storage media with *random access* or *sequential access*? Give a reason for your answer.   **2**

(b) The manager of the shop is going to reduce the price of all products manufactured by Gimballs that cost over £0·50. Describe how the database could be used to produce a list of all the products that will be reduced in price.   **3**

(c) The "Total Value of Stock" field is a *computed field*. What is meant by the term "computed field"?   **1**

(d) Many customers use *electronic funds transfer* at *point of sale* to pay for their shopping.

   (i) Describe the process of electronic funds transfer.   **3**

   (ii) Give **one** reason why many customers prefer this method of payment.   **1**

(e) The individual points of sale are *remote terminals*. From what are the terminals remote?   **1**

	KU	PS

5. Rhona is a computer programmer who works for a company which writes software for schools. She programs using a *high level language*.

(a) Give **one** difference between a high level language and a low level language. — KU 1

(b) (i) When developing the software, what type of *translator* would you suggest that Rhona should use? Give a reason for your answer. — PS 2

   (ii) Name the translator which converts low level language to machine code. — KU 1

(c) Rhona always writes software that is *portable*.

   (i) What is meant by the term "portable"? — KU 1

   (ii) Why is making the software portable an advantage to the company? — PS 1

(d) How does the Copyright, Designs and Patents Act protect Rhona's work? — PS 1

(e) Rhona's programs are very valuable and she does not want to lose any of the work that she has done. What should she do to ensure that none of her software is lost? — PS 2

(f) Rhona tries to develop programs that are *user friendly*.

   (i) To make the software user friendly, should she make the software *command driven* or *menu driven*? Explain your answer. — KU 2

   (ii) State **two** other ways in which software can be made more user friendly. — PS 2

[Turn over for Question 6 on *Page eight*

	KU	PS

6. All computer systems consist of *input devices*, *output devices*, *backing storage devices* and the *central processing unit*.

(*a*) (i) Which part of the central processing unit is responsible for running a program correctly? **1**

  (ii) Which part of the central processing unit carries out calculations and decision-making processes? **1**

(*b*) There are different types of memory in a computer system.

  (i) What type of memory holds the data and instructions while a program is running? **1**

  (ii) What type of memory holds programs that never change? **1**

(*c*) One task of the processor is *resource allocation*. Describe this task. **2**

(*d*) Some computer systems are not *multimedia*. Suggest **one** input device and **one** output device that would be added to a computer system to make it multimedia. **2**

(*e*) (i) When you buy a piece of software, it usually comes on a *CD-ROM*. Give **two** reasons why this medium may be more suitable for this task than using floppy disks. **2**

  (ii) The *operating system* is involved in loading software from the CD-ROM. Name a function of the operating system and describe how it is used in this situation. **2**

[END OF QUESTION PAPER]

[BLANK PAGE]

FOR OFFICIAL USE

G

Total Marks

KU	PS

0560/402

NATIONAL QUALIFICATIONS 2005

THURSDAY, 12 MAY
G/C 9.00 AM – 10.15 AM
F/G 10.20 AM – 11.35 AM

COMPUTING STUDIES
STANDARD GRADE
General Level

Fill in these boxes and read what is printed below.

Full name of centre

Town

Forename(s)

Surname

Date of birth

Day   Month   Year   Scottish candidate number   Number of seat

Read each question carefully.

Attempt **all** questions.

Write your answers in the space provided on the question paper.

Write as neatly as possible.

Answer in sentences wherever possible.

Before leaving the examination room you must give this book to the invigilator. If you do not, you may lose all the marks for this paper.

SCOTTISH
QUALIFICATIONS
AUTHORITY

©

1. Pupils in 1st and 2nd year of a secondary school are going on a team building weekend. The details are stored in a *database*. Below is an example of a *record*.

Name:	Natalya Corrieri
Year:	2nd
House:	Bardowie
Emergency contact:	01334 82566
Medical condition:	Asthma

(a) A parent wants to see the records of all pupils held on this database. Does he have the right to see **all** records?

_____

Explain your answer.

_____

_____

(b) Describe how the guidance teacher would be able to get a *hardcopy* of only those 1st year pupils who are in Bardowie House.

_____

_____

_____

_____

(c) A new pupil has joined the school in 2nd year.

What must be done to include his details in the file?

_____

_____

(d) How can the school prevent unauthorised access to the computerised pupil files?

_____

1. (continued)

(e) The database is held on the school *LAN*.

What do the initials "LAN" stand for?

_____

(f) Some teachers at the school do not know very much about computers. Fortunately the database uses a *Graphical User Interface*. Give **two** reasons why this type of interface is useful for beginners.

1 _____

_____

2 _____

_____

(g) A lot of printing has been done and the Guidance department has been asked to pay towards *running costs*. Give **two** running costs of having the records printed out.

1 _____

2 _____

(h) The guidance teacher makes a second copy which she stores on a floppy disk.

What is this second copy called?

_____

[Turn over

2. A letter is to be sent out to parents telling them what pupils must take on the team building weekend.

   (*a*)   In the letter the year head has been named **many times** as Mrs Smith, whereas it should be Mrs Smythe.

      (i)   Name the feature of a word processing package which is used to make this change.

_____

      (ii) Describe how the feature is used in the above example.

_____

_____

_____

   (*b*)   The letter includes a *standard paragraph* used for all school trips.

      What is a "standard paragraph"?

_____

_____

   (*c*)   Before the secretary prints off the letter he does a *spell check*. It stops every time the year head's name, Mrs Smythe, appears.

      What should he do to prevent this happening?

_____

_____

2. **(continued)**

(*d*) The secretary adds the graphic shown below to the letter.

He then makes changes so it looks like the graphic below.

Which features did he use?

1 _____

2 _____

(*e*) On seeing the letter the year head, Mrs Smythe, decides she would like to swap the last two paragraphs.

How could the secretary do this?

_____

_____

_____

(*f*) When creating the letters for parents both *program* and *data files* are used. Give an example of each type of file in this situation.

(i) Program file _____

(ii) Data file _____

(*g*) How is text represented in a computer system?

_____

[Turn over

3. A *spreadsheet* is kept of the money pupils have saved towards the weekend. From this money they have to pay for an extra trip. Below is part of the spreadsheet.

	A	B	C	D	E	F	G
1	Team Building Weekend						
2							
3	Name	Saved in August	Saved in September	Saved in October	Total Saved	Cost of extra trip	Balance of savings
4	Sally Jones	15	15	20	50	10	40
5	Hilary Smith	10	15	30	55	10	45
6	John Dale	5	10	10	25	10	15
7	Kate Reid	15	5	5	25	10	15
8	David Hill	20	5	10	35	10	25

DO NOT
WRITE IN
THIS MARGIN

KU PS

(a) What formula is used in cell E4?

_____

1
0

(b) What formula is used in cell G4?

_____

_____

1
0

(c) What would have to be done to display all the appropriate figures as money?

_____

_____

2
1
0

(d) The year head wants to include the registration class of each pupil. What must be done to the above table to allow this to happen?

_____

_____

1
0

(e) The spreadsheet is part of an *integrated package*.

What is an "integrated package"?

_____

_____

_____

1
0

3. **(continued)**

(f) Give **one** advantage of the spreadsheet and the database having a similar *HCI*.

_____

_____

1
0

(g) An operating system has several standard functions.   Tick (✓) **two** functions which the operating system would carry out while the spreadsheet was in use.

Loads the data file into the computer ☐

Displays numbers as money ☐

Supplies electricity to the computer ☐

Checks to see which key has been pressed ☐

2
1
0

(h) Why might the year head, Mrs Smythe, want to create a chart from the spreadsheet figures?

_____

_____

1
0

(i) The secretary has used both *online help* and an *online tutorial* for the spreadsheet.

Write whether you think online help or an online tutorial has been used for each of the following.

Introduction lesson

_____

Making a column wider whilst using the program

_____

2
1
0

(j) The spreadsheet is to be printed using a *laser* printer. Give **one** benefit of a laser printer.

_____

1
0

[Turn over

4. Pupils in computing have written a program in Really Basic to help run the tuckshop on the team building weekend. Really Basic is a *high level* language.

(*a*) Give **two** common features of high level languages.

1 _____

_____

2 _____

_____

2
1
0

(*b*) The computer can only understand *machine code*.

What is "machine code"?

_____

_____

1
0

(*c*) The program uses a graphic. Computers represent graphics by a series of tiny dots on the screen.

What are these dots on the screen called?

_____

_____

1
0

(*d*) A pupil called Sarah who has been helping to create the program has difficulty in writing. She uses a voice recognition package to produce text.

(i) What input device is necessary for the voice recognition package?

_____

1
0

(ii) When using it why must she speak clearly?

_____

_____

_____

1
0

(iii) Sarah complains to the teacher that she cannot use all the words she normally does in everyday conversation.

Why can she not use all the words she would like to?

_____

_____

1
0

DO NOT
WRITE IN
THIS MARGIN

KU | PS

4. (continued)

(e) Pupils are to take a computer with them on the team building weekend, to run the tuckshop program.

(i) Suggest a suitable type of computer for this purpose.

_____

(ii) Give a reason for your answer.

_____

_____

[Turn over

10

10

5. Pupils use canoes on the team building weekend which are made on an automated production line that uses *robots*.

(a) Give **two** reasons why you think the production process was automated.

1 _____

_____

2 _____

_____

(b) The various parts of the canoe are brought to the production line by *mobile* robots. The floor gets very dirty.

How can the mobile robots be guided to the correct place?

_____

_____

_____

(c) Suggest one safety precaution that should be taken around mobile robots.

_____

_____

(d) Parts of the production process involves mixing a fast acting glue from two ingredients. A sensor is used to ensure this happens at the correct temperature.

(i) What type of processing should be used for this? Tick (✓) **one** box.

Real time ☐

Batch ☐

Interactive ☐

(ii) Explain your answer.

_____

_____

KU | PS

5. (continued)

(e) The robot arms on the production line can sense if parts are in the correct position for joining together. If they are not, then the parts are repositioned.

(i) Is this an example of an *open* or *closed loop*?

_____

1
0

(ii) Explain your answer.

_____

_____

2
1
0

(f) The sensor is used to measure the level of light.

Is light a *digital* or *analogue* quantity?

_____

1
0

(g) A large amount of data is constantly recorded during the production process and used frequently.

(i) What is the best form of *backing storage* medium for this? Choose from the list below.

CD ROM   *Hard Disk*   *Floppy Disk*   *Magnetic Tape*

_____

1
0

(ii) Give a reason for your answer.

_____

_____

1
0

[Turn over

6. The organisation which provides the team building weekend buys their uniforms from a mail order company. Here is an example of an order form.

Order Form	
Customer Name:	Jessica Murray
Order Number:	3419
Date of Order:	130604
Product Code:	U789
Uniform Size:	32
Quantity:	4

Daily orders are gathered for processing overnight.

(a) (i) What type of processing is the company using?

_____

(ii) Explain your answer.

_____

_____

_____

(b) Checks are carried out by the computer as data is entered from the order form.

Name a field and suggest a suitable check.

Field name _____

Check _____

_____

(c) What type of computer file will the order go into when first received? Tick (✓) **one** box.

Transaction ☐

Master ☐

Backup File ☐

KU | PS

6. **(continued)**

(d) The team building organisation pays the mail order company by cheque. The cheque has *MICR* characters on it.

   (i) What do the initials MICR stand for?

   _____

   1
   0

   (ii) What is **one** advantage of MICR?

   _____

   1
   0

(e) One member of staff of the mail order company works from home.

   Give **one** advantage and **one** disadvantage of working from home.

   Advantage _____

   _____

   Disadvantage _____

   2
   1
   0

   _____

(f) The mail order company sells mailing lists of its customers to other mail order companies. This causes junk mail.

   Give **one** disadvantage of junk mail.

   _____

   1
   0

   _____

[END OF QUESTION PAPER]

[BLANK PAGE]

[BLANK PAGE]

C

0560/403

NATIONAL
QUALIFICATIONS
2005

THURSDAY, 12 MAY
10.35 AM – 12.20 PM

COMPUTING STUDIES
STANDARD GRADE
Credit Level

Read each question carefully.

Attempt **all** questions.

Write your answers in the answer book provided. **Do not** write on the question paper.

Write as neatly as possible.

Answer in sentences wherever possible.

SCOTTISH
QUALIFICATIONS
AUTHORITY

		KU	PS

1. FoneU is a chain of retail outlets that sells mobile phone packages. When a customer purchases a new phone, their details are entered into the company's database. The format of the database is shown below.

Field	Sample Data	Field Size (bytes)
Name	Summers, Heather	30
Address	9 Park Croft	60
Town	Newton	20
Postcode	PH40 3TS	8
Phone Make	Sunyo	15
Phone Model	AS300	5
Phone No	07793030181	12
Network	Talkfone	10

(a)　(i)　What is the maximum number of bytes required to store **one** record of the database? **1**

(ii)　Using your answer from part (i), calculate how many 1·44 Mb floppy disks will be needed to store 10,000 records.
Show all of your working. **4**

(b)　As the *data user*, the manager of FoneU has to comply with the *Data Protection Act* of 1998.

(i)　Give **two** requirements of the Data Protection Act with which the data user must comply. **2**

(ii)　Give **two** rights that the *data subjects* have under this legislation. **2**

(c)　The sales manager wishes to send a *standard letter* to all customers living in Newtown who are on the Talkfone network.

(i)　What is a standard letter? **2**

(ii)　Describe how the database could be used to produce a list of Talkfone customers living in Newtown. **3**

(iii)　What is the name given to the process of using a computer to insert the customers' details from the database into the standard letter in a single operation? **1**

	KU	PS

2. SubSea Contractors own a fleet of ships that are used to service oilrigs. One of their main tasks is to transfer drinking water from the ship's tanks to the oilrig. This is a computerised system, with software used to control the action of the ship's water pumps.

(a) Give **one** advantage of using a computerised system rather than a manual system in this case. — KU: 1

(b) Information about the water level is fed back to the system and the water pumps slow down, then stop when the water levels have reached a certain limit.

   (i) What do we call a device that is used to provide *feedback*? — KU: 1

   (ii) The water levels vary continuously. What must be done to ensure that the water level readings are in a form that the computer system can process? — PS: 1

   (iii) What type of control loop is used in this situation? — PS: 1

(c) The software was written using a *control language* and is stored on *ROM chips*.

   (i) Give **one** reason why a control language was used for this system. — PS: 1

   (ii) Although ROM chips are the most expensive way of storing programs, give **two** reasons why this storage medium is used here. — PS: 2

(d) Workers onboard ship contact their families using *e-mail* on the ship's computer system. Which **two** of the following statements are true?

   A A piece of software called a modem is needed for Internet access.
   B ISPs can provide e-mail accounts.
   C The computer's operating system is **not** involved in Internet access.
   D Communications and Browser software is needed for Internet access. — KU: 2

(e) This computer, like all others, has a *Central Processing Unit* (CPU) containing an *ALU* and a *Control Unit*.

   Explain the purpose of:

   (i) the ALU; — KU: 2

   (ii) the Control Unit. — KU: 1

[Turn over

	KU	PS

3. A Young Enterprise group hopes to raise money by selling two types of customised T-shirt. They use a spreadsheet to calculate what customers spend on their products.

Part of the spreadsheet is shown below.

	A	B	C	D	E	F
1	**Discount is**	20%				
2						
3	Name	T-shirt 1	T-shirt 2	Total	Discount	Final Cost
4	Kelly, J	10.00	5.00	15.00	3.00	12.00
5	Patel, R	3.00	7.00	10.00	0.00	10.00
6	McLean, A	3.00	3.00	6.00	0.00	6.00
7	Winters, H	8.00	3.00	11.00	2.20	8.80
8						
9						

(a) Cell **D4** contains a formula to calculate the total amount owed. It has been *replicated* into cells **D5**, **D6** and **D7**.

  (i) What is meant by the term "replicate"?

  (ii) Which type of *referencing* would have been used to replicate this formula?

(b) If customers spend over £10, then a discount of 20% is given. Cell **E4** uses a formula to calculate any discount due.

  (i) Write down a suitable formula for cell **E4** **which includes** cell **B1**.

  (ii) Before this formula was replicated down column **E**, one of the cells in the formula required an *absolute reference*. Which cell?

  (iii) What could be done to prevent the formula in this column from being altered unintentionally?

(c) The *cell attributes* of **B4** to **F7** are to be changed.

  (i) What is meant by the term cell attributes?

  (ii) Suggest a suitable alteration to the cell attributes.

(d) Every month the Young Enterprise group produces a word processed report showing sales for that month. It includes a table similar to that shown above. Should *static* or *dynamic data linkage* be used in this case? Justify your answer.

KU marks: (a)(i) 1; (c)(i) 1

PS marks: (a)(ii) 1; (b)(i) 4; (b)(ii) 1; (b)(iii) 1; (c)(ii) 1; (d) 2

			KU	PS

4. MegaTrain is a call-centre company that sells thousands of tickets each day for train journeys throughout the UK. Each employee uses a *remote terminal* connected to a mainframe computer at the company's head office in Manchester. This computer has a large database that holds information about the trains and ticket availability. Employees use this database to inform customers of prices and book seats when required.

An excerpt from the database is shown below.

Train Code	Depart	Destination	Total Seats	Seats Sold	Seats Available
31243	Waverley	Queen Street	350	295	55
31255	Waverley	Kings Cross	800	451	349
32453	Central	Euston	800	704	96

(a) The value in the field "Seats Available" is automatically generated by the computer. What name is given to this type of field? **1**

(b) The last digit in the field "Train Code" is a *check digit*.

    (i) What is the purpose of a check digit? **1**

    (ii) From what data is the check digit calculated? **1**

(c) Should this database be stored on *random (direct) access* backing storage media or *sequential access* backing storage media? Explain your answer. **2**

(d) MegaTrain makes daily backup copies of the database. Three generations of backup are kept. Describe this backup process. (You may use a diagram.) **3**

(e) The mainframe computer allows *multi-access* from its remote terminals.

    (i) What is a remote terminal? **1**

    (ii) Explain what is meant by the term multi-access. **2**

    (iii) Why is a multi-access system required at MegaTrain? **1**

(f) MegaTrain customers generally pay for their tickets over the phone using *electronic funds transfer* (*EFT*).

What steps are involved in the process of electronic funds transfer? **3**

(g) Morven, an employee at MegaTrain, has poor eyesight. The *HCI parameters* of her remote terminal have been altered to make it easier for her to see what is on the screen.

Describe **two** ways in which the parameters may have been changed. **2**

[Turn over

	KU	PS

5. Ben has his own business, selling classroom resources to teachers. He needs software to help him construct letters and calculate his expenditure.

(a) He is unsure whether to buy an *integrated package* or separate *general purpose packages*.

Give **two** reasons why he may decide to buy separate general purpose packages.

$\hspace{20cm}$ PS: 2

(b) Before he makes his purchase, Ben has to ensure his computer is capable of running the new software.

Name **two** features of his computer system that he will have to check to see whether it is able to run this software.

PS: 2

(c) Ben has designed a unique company logo for all his correspondence.

Name the legislation that makes copying Ben's work, without his permission, an offence.

KU: 1

(d) Some of his products are software packages that teachers can use for training purposes. They are distributed to schools on *CD-ROM*. He has tried to make these products as *user friendly* as possible by including *online help* and *online tutorials*.

(i) What is online help?

KU: 1

(ii) What is an online tutorial?

KU: 1

(iii) He has also designed the software so that it is *portable*.

What is meant by the term portable?

KU: 1

(iv) Give **two** reasons for using CD-ROM as a distribution medium.

KU: 2

(e) Ben has bought a new computer. The *operating system* offers *multi-programming* and efficient *resource allocation*.

(i) What is meant by the term multi-programming?

KU: 2

(ii) Why is resource allocation an essential role of the operating system?

PS: 2

(iii) Another role of the operating system is to manage *main memory*.

How does the operating system locate items in main memory?

PS: 2

[END OF QUESTION PAPER]

[BLANK PAGE]

[BLANK PAGE]

[BLANK PAGE]

[BLANK PAGE]

[BLANK PAGE]

[BLANK PAGE]

[BLANK PAGE]

[BLANK PAGE]

Pocket answer section for
SQA General and Credit Computing Studies
2001 – 2005

© 2005 Scottish Qualifications Authority, All Rights Reserved
Published by Leckie & Leckie Ltd, 8 Whitehill Terrace, St Andrews, Scotland, KY16 8RN
tel: 01334 475656, fax: 01334 477392, enquiries@leckieandleckie.co.uk, www.leckieandleckie.co.uk

Computing Studies
General Level
2001

1. (a)
- The graphic has been resized (1 mark)
- And rotated (1 mark)

(b) 1 mark for each of any of the answers below (maximum of 2 marks):
- Size of text
- Text has been emboldened
- Font has been changed

(c) The lines of text have been selected (1 mark), And then right aligned (1 mark)

(d) (i) 1 mark for each of any of the answers below (maximum of 1 mark):
- Poor quality of printout
- Printer is slow
- Printer is noisy

(ii) 1 mark for each of any of the answers below (maximum of 1 mark):
- Printer is cheaper to buy
- Colour is available at a low cost

(e) (i) One package containing several components (word processor, spreadsheet, database, graphics, etc) (1 mark)
AND
1 mark for each of any of the answers below (maximum of 1 mark):
- which allow easy transfer of data from one component to another
- which have a common HCI between parts

(ii) Interaction of computer, and user is done through using icons (1 mark) to represent hardware and software (1 mark)

(f) Either with correct explanation
On-line help because this is designed so that she can search or pick out the required information without leaving the package.
On-line tutorial where she can focus on a lesson or part of a lesson which covers the area in which she needs help.

2. (a) Set the cell format attributes to 2 decimal places

(b) Set to currency format

(c) =F16–C16

(d) =SUM (C2:C14) **or** other correct answers involving SUM

(e) (i) Insert a row (1 mark)
Between 6 and 7 and enter details (1 mark)

2. (ii) 1 mark for each of any of the answers below (maximum of 1 mark):
- Alter cell/column width to fit text
- Use text wrap
- Any other suitable answer

3. (a) Local Area Network

(b) (i) Backing storage—storage capacity for retrieving saved files
Backup—a second copy of data in case the original is lost or damaged

(ii) Hard disk—because of fast access and large capacity

(iii) 1 mark for each of any of the answers below (maximum of 2 marks):
- CD ROM—read only
- tape—access too slow
- floppy disk—limited capacity

(c) 1 mark for each of any of the answers below (maximum of 2 marks):
- Keep secure
- not store any longer than required
- restrict access

(d) Modem

4. (a) (i) Sort (1 mark)
On the age field in low-to-high order (1 mark)

(ii) Search (1 mark)
On the age field for <13 (1 mark)

(b) Create new record and enter the details

(c) Create an extra field (1 mark)
To enter email address (1 mark)
(or logical field [1 mark] indicating whether or not they have email [1 mark])

5. (a) 1 mark for each of any of the answers below (maximum of 2 marks):
- More flexible hours
- No travelling, saving time/fuel costs
- Less pollution

(b) 1 mark for each of any of the answers below (maximum of 1 mark):
- Less Social contact
- Lack of motivation
- Breakdown of technology could cause problems etc

(c) Manual jobs—computers will do more of the manual tasks **or** example

(d) 1 mark for each of any of the answers below (maximum of 1 mark):
- People will not have access to information
- not get the best financial deals

Computing Studies
General Level
2001 (cont.)

6. (a) Systems analyst
Looks at the way a company works (1 mark)
And suggests hardware and software (1 mark)

Programmer
Writes coding to user's requirements (1 mark)
Recommends commercial software (1 mark)

Data preparation operator
Person who enters data into a computer system (1 mark)
And verifies data entry (1 mark)

(b) (i) FILE 1—transaction file
FILE 2—master file

(ii) Batch

(c) (i) 1 mark for each of any of the answers below (maximum of 1 mark):
- Running costs: paper/toner/updating hardware/updating software
- Training costs
- Repairs

(ii) 1 mark for each of any of the answers below (maximum of 1 mark):
- Less staff needed—lower wages
- Company more competitive

(d) Double entry
range/length/reliability checks/use of check digits

(e) Either yes or no but must explain answer:

YES   Because documents are stored electronically (1 mark)
Reducing the need for paper copies (1 mark)

NO   Because the use of computers has resulted in an explosion of information (1 mark)
Leading to more hard copy of documents, e-mail, mail shots etc (1 mark)

(f) (i) A storage medium which is like an acetate sheet on which is stored data in micro form (1 mark)
The microfiche is not read by a computer. It is read by a kind of magnifying system using a light source. (1 mark)

(ii) 1 mark for each of any of the answers below (maximum of 1 mark):
- Cannot be edited
- Requires special equipment to read it

7. (a) 1 mark for each of any of the answers below (maximum of 2 marks):
- No one hurt if crash
- Less expense
- Less pollution
- Try out extreme conditions

7. (b) (i) The data which is input is processed immediately

(ii) 1 mark for each of any of the answers below (maximum of 1 mark):
- Reaction of learner eg turning the steering wheel, must be in real time to be effective
- Reactions of users would not be assessed accurately

(c) Analogue (1 mark)
Because the turning of the wheel is continuously varying (1 mark)

(d) Screen/virtual reality headset (1 mark)
Used to display output in a visual form (1 mark)
OR
Printer (1 mark)
To print out hard copy of test results, etc (1 mark)

Computing Studies
Credit Level 2001

1. (a) 1 mark for each of any of the answers below (maximum of 2 marks):
   - Modem
   - Telephone/ISDN line
   - Communications software
   - Browser
   - Dial-up software
   - Internet provider

   (b) (i) 1 mark for each of any of the answers below (maximum of 2 marks):
      - Have a choice of application packages
      - Common HCI
      - Ease of transfer of data
      - Dynamic linkage
      - Less expensive to buy compared to individual application packages
      - Less memory needed to run
      - Less backing storage needed

      (ii) 1 mark for each of any of the answers below (maximum of 2 marks):
      - May be less powerful than a stand-alone package
      - More memory needed
      - Redundant packages

   (c) 1 mark for each of any of the answers below (maximum of 2 marks):
   - Large monitor
   - Magnifying screen on monitor
   - Enlarge font

   (d) (i) Data Protection Act
      (ii) Gurmeet

   (e) 1.44MB = 1.44 * 1024 * 1024 bytes
       = 1509949 bytes (1 mark)

       Number of customer records
       = 1509949/500 (1 mark)
       = 3019 (1 mark)

   (f) Search (1 mark)
       On Country field = UK (1 mark)
       Complex sort the result on Town field in alphabetical order (1 mark)
       AND Total Spent field from highest to lowest (1 mark)

2. (a) Relative

   (b) (i) =IF (D3>200, D3*B9, 0)
       (1 mark will be deducted for each error/omission)

      (ii) B9

   (c) Protect/lock cells

   (d) 1 mark for each of any of the answers below (maximum of 1 mark):
   - Colour of text
   - Menu or command driven
   - Size of text
   - Speed of mouse within the program.

2. (e) (i) 1 mark for each of any of the answers below (maximum of 1 mark):
      - Style or formatting applied to the cell
      - Contents/appearance of contents of cells

      (ii) Alter to currency (£)

   (f) 1 mark for each of any of the answers below (maximum of 1 mark):
   - Very slow to install software
   - Storage of large number of disks could be difficult
   - Time consuming
   - More easily corrupted

3. (a) (i) 1 mark for each of any of the answers below (maximum of 2 marks):
      - Bump sensor
      - Proximity sensor
      - Infra-red

      (ii) Closed loop (1 mark)
       1 mark for each of any of the answers below (maximum of 1 mark):
      - There are sensors
      - There is feedback
      - Robot will react to the situation.

   (b) (i) The part that fits on the end of the arm.

      (ii) 1 mark for each of any of the answers below (maximum of 1 mark):
      - Brush
      - Hose
      - Nozzle

   (c) (i) 1 mark for each of any of the answers below (maximum of 1 mark):
      - Language more suited to controlling the robot
      - Programming robot easier as necessary syntax available.

      (ii) 1 mark for each of any of the answers below (maximum of 1 mark):
      - Loads instantly
      - Less liable to corruption
      - Cannot be easily erased accidentally or deliberately.

   (d) 1 mark for each of any of the answers below (maximum of 1 mark):
   - Assembler
   - Interpreter
   - Compiler.

4. (a) 32 bits

   (b) The computer allocates a unique address to each memory location in the main memory.

   (c) (i) Multi-programming means that more than 1 program (1 mark)
       Can run at the same time (1 mark)

      (ii) 1 mark for each of any of the answers below (maximum of 1 mark):
      - Can move easily and quickly between applications
      - Can have different applications open in different windows

Computing Studies
Credit Level 2001 (cont.)

4. (c) (ii) continued
- Can view data in different applications at the same time
- Time saved by not having to close an application before opening another.

(d) 1 mark for each of any of the answers below (maximum of 1 mark):
- Can hear sounds instead of just reading the text
- Can input sounds or music/video/pictures.

(e) (i) Binary code unique to each letter or a named example eg ASCII.

(ii) Floating point representation (**or** mantissa and exponent).

5. (a) (i) 1 mark for each of any of the answers below (maximum of 1 mark):
- To ensure that the data is valid
- To check that the data has been entered correctly.

(ii) It is calculated from the other digits.

(iii) Recalculation and checking with check digit.

(b) (i) Technique which allows characters to be read into the computer via a scanner.

(ii) 1 mark for each of any of the answers below (maximum of 2 marks):
- Handwritten or typed reports can be quickly entered into the computer.
- Handwritten or typed reports can be accurately entered into the computer.
- Text entered this way can be edited in a word processor.

(c) Three generations (grandparent/parent/child) (1 mark)
1 mark for each of any of the answers below (maximum of 1 mark):
- Most common model used
- Two generations is too few, four generations is too many

(d) (i) Computer Misuse Act

(ii) Hacking

(iii) Discourages illegal copying of software.

(e) 1 mark for each of any of the answers below (maximum of 2 marks):
- Less delay likely when orders processed
- Can get immediate update of account
- Know immediately if game is in stock
- Can order other game if first choice not in stock
- Speed of processing.

6. (a) (i) A letter which can be used again and again (1 mark)
With parts that are personalised (1 mark)

(ii) Datafile with fields/data to be merged.

6. (b) (i) A piece of software

(ii) Allows the printer and the computer to communicate.

(c) (i) Computed or calculated field

(ii) Multiply the field "ticket cost" (1 mark)
By the field "number required" (1 mark)

(d) (i) Select area to be charted (1 mark)
Select charting option (1 mark)

(ii) Dynamic

(e) Header

Computing Studies
General Level 2002

1. (*a*) (i) 1 mark for each of any of the answers below (maximum of 1 mark):
- Cut and paste
- Move
- Drag and drop

    (ii) Select/highlight paragraph (1 mark)
AND
CUT and PASTE at new position
(1 mark)
OR
Move to its new position (1 mark)
OR
DRAG and DROP at new position
(1 mark)

(*b*) (i) 1 mark for each of any of the answers below (maximum of 1 mark):
- Search and replace
- Find and change

    (ii) Search for "McNeish" (1 mark)
replace with "Brown" (1 mark)

(*c*) 1 mark for each of any of the answers below (maximum of 1 mark):
- Pre-typed block of text
- Text which can be placed automatically where required in document

(*d*) Sam saves time typing out the text of the paragraph each time (1 mark)
Sam does not need to check the content carefully as each standard paragraph will have been carefully checked already (1 mark)

(*e*) 1 mark for each of any of the answers below (maximum of 2 marks):
- Use of passwords
- different users have different levels of access
- keep computers in locked (secure) rooms
- encrypt files

(*f*) 1 mark for each of any of the answers below (maximum 1 mark):
- buying floppy discs
- printer paper (1 mark)/ink for printer
- electricity
- internet connections
- updating software
- maintenance

2. (*a*) (i) =C2*D2 (2 marks, deduct 1 mark for each error)

    (ii) =SUM(E2:E5) (2 marks, deduct 1 mark for each error)
OR
=E2+E3+E4+E5 (2 marks, deduct 1 mark for each error)

2. (*b*) 1 mark for each of any of the answers below (maximum of 1 mark):
- replication
- fill down
- copy and paste

(*c*) Select cells (any row from 2 to 6) (1 mark)/ insert a new row OR insert cells (1 mark)

(*d*) Alter column width

(*e*) EITHER
Alter cell attributes/format . . . (1 mark)
. . . to display as currency (1 mark)
OR
Select cells (1 mark)
Format as currency (1 mark)

(*f*) 1 mark for each of any of the answers below (maximum of 2 marks):
- Ease of data transfer from spreadsheet to word processor
- Cheaper than buying seperate packages
- common user interface
- has all the facilities to do the job in a single package

(*g*) (i) On-line tutorial

    (ii) 1 mark for each of any of the answers below (maximum of 1 mark):
- an on-line tutorial introduces beginners to the basic features of a piece of software
- on-line help is for someone who knows the basics but has a specific problem to solve
- a tutorial teaches how to use the package step by step

3. (*a*)
- Sort (1 mark)
- On height field (1 mark)
- In descending order or "high to low" (1 mark)

(*b*)
- Search/final/query/filter (1 mark)
- field "colour of flower" has value "Purple"
(AND)
- field "flowering month(s)" includes value "April" (1 mark)

(*c*) (i) Menu driven

    (ii) 1 mark for each of any of the answers below (maximum of 1 mark):
- Do not need to remember commands
- Do not need to learn commands
- Do not need to type in commands
- Less likely to make errors

(*d*)
- Scanner (1 mark)
- digital camera (1 mark)

(*e*) 1 mark for each of any of the answers below (maximum of 1 mark):
- Scale graphic
- Resize
- Drag handles

Computing Studies
General Level 2002 (cont.)

4. (a) Wide Area Network

   (b) Field name eg Time received or any other suitable (1 mark)

   Appropriate range eg Time received must be between 0000 and 2359 (1 mark)

   (c) 1 mark for each of any of the answers below (maximum of 1 mark):
   - Real Time
   - Interactive

   (d) A digit <u>calculated</u> from the other digits (1 mark)
   If any digit entered incorrectly, you get a different check digit on recalculation so <u>error is detected</u> (1 mark)

   (e) (i) Batch processing
   (ii) Parcel Number order

   (f) (i) 1 mark for each of any of the answers below (maximum of 1 mark):
   - Palmtop
   - PPA
   - hand held

   (ii) 1 mark for each of any of the answers below (maximum of 1 mark):
   - Stylus
   - Pressure sensitive screen
   - Write on screen with special pen

5. (a) (i) 1 mark for each of any of the answers below (maximum of 1 mark):
   - High or initial cost
   - (Cost of) laying off workers
   - Cost of retraining workers

   (ii) 1 mark for each of any of the answers below (maximum of 1 mark):
   - Better accuracy/quality of production
   - Lower running costs
   - Long term savings
   - Lower wage bill

   (b) 1 mark for each of any of the answers below (maximum of 2 marks):
   - Sensors on robots—touch someone, will stop
   - Warning lights or buzzers on robots
   - Putting robots in cages
   - Separate working areas

   (c) (i) Closed loop control
   (ii) Robot needs <u>feedback</u> (1 mark) from <u>sensor</u> to know that the window is gripped (1 mark)

   (d) (i) Analogue
   (ii) 1 mark for each of any of the answers below (maximum of 1 mark):
   - Amount of light varies continuously
   - Amount of light varies over many different values

5. (e) 1 mark for each of any of the answers below (maximum of 1 mark):
   - magnetic guide
   - light guide
   - accept programmed to remember
   - follow a white line

6. (a) 1 mark for each of any of the answers below (maximum of 2 marks):
   - English-like language
   - Problem orientated
   - Needs translation
   - Portable
   - Uses standard arithmetic functions
   - Easy to detect errors
   - Easy to edit

   (b) (i) 1 mark for each of any of the answers below (maximum of 1 mark):
   - Contains instructions to carry out a task
   - Files that can be run/executable

   (ii) 1 mark for each of any of the answers below (maximum of 1 mark):
   - Contains data to be processed by a program
   - Used by a program file
   - A collection of data
   - Used to store data

   (c) (i) Random Accesss Memory (1 mark)
   (ii) 1 mark for each of any of the answers below (maximum of 1 mark):
   - ROM cannot have its contents changed while RAM can
   - cannot load into ROM

   (d) HELLO (2 marks)

   (e) 1 mark for each of any of the answers below (maximum of 1 mark):
   Any two of the following:
   - A "1" represents a black dot/pixel/square
   - A "0" represents a white dot/pixel (allow vice-versa)
   - Correct picture (allow 1 pixel error)

   (f) 1 mark for each of any of the answers below (maximum of 2 marks):
   - Take input data from input devices
   - Give output to output devices
   - Handle filing system
   - Memory management
   - Other valid suggestion
   - Boot PC

   (g) 1 mark for each of any of the answers below (maximum of 1 mark):
   Any two of the following:
   - Smaller "footprint" on desk
   - Less radiation
   - Less power to run it
   - Better contrast
   - Flatter display
   - Clearer image
   - Less glare
   - Less eye strain

6. (*h*) (i) 1 mark for each of any of the answers below (maximum of 1 mark):
- Voice (recognition)
- Headset/microphone/blow pipe

(ii) 1 mark for each of any of the answers below (maximum of 1 mark):
- Slower, less accurate
- Takes time to teach the system your voice pattern

Computing Studies
Credit Level 2002

1. (*a*) Search/Filter/Query database (1 mark)
Colour = "black" (1 mark)
AND Height > 15 (1 mark)

(*b*) Sort on the height field (1 mark)
And then name field (1 mark)

(*c*) (i) 128 bytes

(ii) Using 1 Mb = 1024 x 1024 bytes
1.44 Mb = 1509949.44 bytes
No of records = 1509949.44 ÷ 128*

= 11796.48

Using 1 Mb = 1000 x 1000
1.44 Mb = 1440000 bytes
No of records = 1440000 ÷ 128*

= 11250

* or answer to part (i) above

(iii) Random (or direct) access (1 mark)

(*d*) (i) 1 mark for each of any of the bullets below (maximum of 2 marks):
- Obtain and process the data fairly and lawfully
- Register the purposes for which they hold it
- Not use or disclose the information in a way contrary to these purposes
- Hold only information which is adequate, relevant and not excessive for the purposes
- Hold only accurate information
- Keep it up to date
- Ensure data held is up to date
- Not keep the information any longer than necessary
- Give individuals access to information about themselves, and where appropriate correct or erase the information
- Take appropriate security measures

(ii) 1 mark for each of any of the bullets below (maximum of 2 marks):
- To check to see if an organisation holds information about you.
- To see a copy of the data.
- To have any incorrect or out of date data amended.
- Right of compensation for misuse of personal data.

2. (*a*) (i) Conditional (IF) formula (1 mark)

(ii) Relative referencing (1 mark)
As the formula is copied down the column the cell references have to change to refer to cells in the correct row (1 mark)

(iii) Use of cell protection/locking

(*b*) (i) Validation

Computing Studies
Credit Level 2002 (cont.)

2. (*b*) continued

    (ii) 1 mark for each of any of the bullets below (maximum of 1 mark):
- Verification checks that something is correct whereas validation checks that something is sensible.
- Human does verification/computer validation

(*c*)   (i) A printer driver

    (ii) 1 mark for each of any of the bullets below (maximum of 1 mark):
- Allows printer and computer to communicate
- Ensures printout is correct/as it appears on screen

(*d*) 1 mark for each of any of the bullets below (maximum of 2 marks):
- Dynamic data linkage
- The table in the report would be updated automatically each month.

(*e*) 1 mark for each of any of the bullets below (maximum of 2 marks):
- Use of a GUI—icon easy to remember
- Menu-driven, user do not have to remember commands, avoids mistyping reports
- Use of WIMP system—Windows, Icons and Menus used with a mouse controlled pointer
- On-line help built into the program so that the user can get assistance without having to leave the package

3. (*a*) (Data can be input, outputted and stored using) a variety of different data
OR
such as text, graphic, audio, video, etc

(*b*)   (i) Each storage location has its own unique (1 mark)
address (1 mark)

    (ii) Floating point representation

    (iii) The number is split into two parts (1 mark)
The mantissa and the exponent (1 mark)

(*c*) 1 mark for each of any of the bullets below (maximum of 2 marks):
- Input/output management
- Memory management
- Backing store management
- File management
- Scheduling
- error reporting
- resource allocater

3. (*d*) 1 mark for each of any of the bullets below (maximum of 2 marks):
- The word size is the number of bits the computer can process in a single operation
- Width of a databus/bits transferred in 1 cycle

(*e*) 1 mark for each of any of the bullets below (maximum of 2 marks):
- Common HCI—easier to learn
- Can have several different documents open at the same time
- Easy to transfer data between different documents
- Cheaper than buying lots of different individual GPPs
- Easier to install
Takes up less disk space

4. (*a*) A systems analysis

(*b*) Either of the following:
Programming (1 mark)
Instructions entered into the computer (1 mark)
OR
Lead through (1 mark)
Robot . . . memory (1 mark)

(*c*) 1 mark for each of any of the bullets below (maximum of 2 marks):
- Software cannot be deleted or changed
- Software loads very quickly
- Memory retained when power is switched off
- Does not need to be loaded each time

(*d*)   (i) 1 mark for each of any of the bullets below (maximum of 1 mark)
- System reacts to outside conditions
- Idea of feedback causing reaction in this case

    (ii) Data must be converted from analogue to digital or be digitised

(*e*) 1 mark for each of any of the bullets below (maximum of 2 marks):
- Robots do not need holidays
- Work in extreme conditions
- Reduces chance of human error
- Saves on wages
- Speed with good explanation
- Increased safety
- Work of good quality
- Any suitable

5. (*a*) A terminal away from the processor

(*b*) Hard disk (1 mark)
AND
Fast, direct (random) access (1 mark)
OR
Large enough to hold a lot of data (1 mark)

(*c*)   (i) Many people can use the processor (1 mark)
at the same time (1 mark)

5. (c) (ii) People will be buying tickets at the same time in different shops.

(d) Most recent back-up is the son (1 mark)
Son becomes father, father becomes grandfather (1 mark)
Grandfather deleted and now new son saved (idea of rotation) (1 mark)

(e) 1 mark for each of any of the bullets below (maximum of 1 mark):
- Speed of printing
- Saving in printer ink/toner
- Standardisation of tickets

(f) (i) A letter sent to many people with the only difference being the personal details

(ii) Mail merge

(iii) 1 mark for each of any of the bullets below (maximum of 1 mark):
- Speed of printing
- High quality

6. (a) A portable program can be used on different machine types.

(b) (i) Assemblers translate low level, (assembly) language

(ii) **Reason for**:
Any one from the following:
Interpreters are good for finding errors in programs
Because program is being developed
Ease of editing errors
Any other valid reason

Reason against:
Interpreters have to translate the program every time it is run, so the programs run more slowly (and take up more memory than compiled programs).

(c) 1 mark for each of any of the bullets below (maximum of 2 marks):
- increase size of icons/fonts/cursor
- change the contrast
- colour scheme
- resolution
- any suitable

(d) The Computer Misuse Act

(e) (i) 1 mark for each of any of the bullets below (maximum of 3 marks):
- Many people can access files simultaneously
- Files can be accessed from any location
- Data can be kept secure with use of user names and passwords
- Data and programs can be transferred between stations on the network
- Sharing peripherals
- Sharing data held centrally
- Internet mail
- Activities can be monitored

6. (e) (ii) 1 mark for each of any of the bullets below (maximum of 2 marks):
- All users have (usernames and) passwords
- That have different levels of access
- Prevent physical access to computers on the network

Computing Studies
General Level 2003

1. (a) Paragraph used again and again
Pre-prepared text
OR
Text stored as file on disk and placed in
document as required

(b) (i) Use Search and Replace OR Find and
Change Or mixture
NOT spell check as 'cocoa' is a correct
spelling

(ii) Searching for 'Cocoa',
Replacing with 'Coco'

(c) Any one from:
- Don't have to type each individual
invitation
- Easy to correct mistakes
- Can save work
- Print multiple copies
- other valid answers

(d) Spell check finds word 'MacKay'
Because real/people's names [not in its
dictionary]

(e) Because 'hops' is a correct spelling
OR
Because the word 'hops' is in its dictionary

(f) Use PRINT FROM ____ TO ____
With correct range ie 3 TO 5
eg Open dialogue box. Print from 3 to 5
OR
Selecting pages ie 3, 4 and 5
Entered at appropriate stage (print dialogue
box)
OR
Select text in pages
Print selection
OR
Clear explanation of appropriate method
OR
Accept copy & paste into new document and
then print

2. (a) (i) Any one from:
- Laptop
- Palmtop
- Tablet Computer
- Pocket Computer

(ii) Any one from:
- Portability
- (laptop) screen is larger than a palmtop
- (palmtop) more portable than a desktop
- Other valid answer

(b) Any one from:
- (=) B4 * C4
- SUM (B4 * C4)

(c) Any one from:
- (=)SUM(D4:D7)
- (=)SUM(D4..D7)
- (=)D4+D5+D6+D7
- function (ie SUM or '+')
- SUM B4:B7
- range (ie D4 to D7)

2. (d) (i) Replicated from D4 [Can replicate upwards
from D7]
(ii) Into D5, D6, D7 OR
down to D7

(e) INSERT a new ROW
At rows 4, 5, 6 OR 7
Or move totals down one (a row)
Move totals down only 1

(f) Select cells in column D
Choose "Currency" option OR
Change the attributes/format

(g) (i) Any one from:
- More features in full package
- No need to pay for (say) graphics software
which he does not need
- Cheaper than buying an integrated package
- Other valid answers

(ii) - Other GPPs in integrated package eg
word processor, database
- Common HCI for all integrated GPPs
- Cheaper than buying a range of
application packages
- Ease of transferring data between packages
- Other valid answers

3. (a) Sort
On the "(Last) Name" field

(b) Search/find/filter/query
For the word "Fishing" in field "interests"
[AND] "June" is contained in the "Months
Visiting" field

(c) Any two of the following:
- Physical security (eg locked doors)
- Usernames and Passwords (accept
'passwords')
- Encryption
- Other valid answers

(d) (i) Data Protection Act or DPA
(ii) Any two from:
- Register (with the Data Protection
Registrar)
- Only use data for registered purposes
- Keep data up-to-date
- Other valid answers

(e) Any two from:
- Paper for printer
- Toner/ink for printer
- Floppy disks
- Electricity
- Other valid answers

4. (a) WAN or Wide Area Network

(b) Any two from:
- Has to process large amounts of data
- Has to process data quickly
- Requires multiple access
- Any other suitable answer

4. (c) An extra digit at the end of the number
OR
A digit calculated from the rest of the digits

Used to detect errors at data entry
OR
Used to validate data

(d) (i) Batch processing
(ii) Processing delayed
OR
All data processed together
OR
Processed at night

(e) Turnaround document

(f) • Systems Analyst
Investigates how company's old system
works (without computers)
OR
Recommends hardware and software
OR
Specifies new software

• Computer Operator
Looks after day to day needs of large
computer system
OR
Organises the running of batch programs,
backups

• Data Preparation Operator
Enters data (from paper forms into the
system)
OR
Deals with validation errors in data entry

5. (a) Any two from:
• Mobile robots have sirens, lights
• Fixed robots are in cages to separate them
from the workers
• If moving robot senses something in the
way it is programmed to stop

(b) (i) Closed loop control
(ii) Robot uses feedback from sensor to know
how much has been picked up
OR
Allow marks for "feedback"

(c) Any two from:
• Has had to be retrained
• Works less hours
• Works in repair or programming robots
• Has more leisure time
• Other possible valid answers

(d) Any two from:
• Less cost compared to using real fireworks
to see effect
• Less time to set up a simulation compared
to setting out display
• Less danger from fireworks going wrong
• Previewing the display of combination
fireworks
• Any other valid answer

6. (a) Any two from:
• Handle input from input devices
• Send output to output devices
• Manage the filing system (disc storage)
• Manage HCI
• Other valid answers

(b) Any two from:
• Find commands in menus
• ICONS represent documents etc
• Windows are used to represent different
folders/documents
• Other valid answers

(c) Scanner
OR
Digital camera
OR
Webcam

(d) (i) Program files contain the instructions
telling the computer what to do

(ii) Data files store information for programs to
work on
OR
Data files store information and are created
by programs

(e) (i) Customers who are blind or have limited
vision can have the computer read out
pages of text to them
OR
Other valid answer
(ii) Loudspeaker
OR
Headphones

(f) Handwriting recognition does not store the
shape of the signature
OR
Because it tries to convert written characters
into typed characters
OR
Doesn't have the correct hardware/software

7. (a) Full set of all characters which the computer
can store/process
OR
The letters, digits, punctuation characters the
computer handles

(b) Computer/processor only actually 'understands'
(machine code)

(c) (i) RAM
(ii) RAM can have its contents altered to store
user data
OR
You cannot store programs in ROM
OR
ROM has fixed contents

(d) (i) Hard disc drive
(ii) Magnetic tape drive

Computing Studies
General Level 2003 (cont.)

7. (*e*) (i) Kenneth can run more programs at once
OR
Kenneth can run larger programs
OR
System may run more quickly
OR
Other valid answer

(ii) Kenneth's programs will run more quickly
OR
Other valid answers
OR
System will run more quickly
OR
Supports multimedia applications

Computing Studies
Credit Level 2003

1. (*a*) (i) Many users have access to the network
At the same time

(ii) Many customers across all branches need to be served (at the same time)

(*b*) (i) Making sure that data entry is correct

(ii) Double entry (or a description of double entry method)

(*c*) (i) The Computer Misuse Act

(ii) Any one from
• (The creation (and/or distribution) of) computer viruses
• altering/changing files
• computer fraud

(iii) Any one from:
• Prevent physical access by putting computers in secured rooms
• Use of firewalls
• Encryption
• Biometric methods

(*d*) (i) Real time
OR
Interactive

(ii) Any one from:
• Balances are kept up-to-date
• Customers find it easier to avoid going overdrawn

(iii) Random (direct) access

(*e*) (i) Scanner/optical character reader

(ii) The notion of the text/image being scanned/read
The notion of this being interpreted/changed into text
Matching to other characters

(iii) Text will only be recognised if it is written clearly/easy for computer to read/computer can't read joined up writing

2. (*a*) • Search (accept Filter/Find/Query) City = "Edinburgh"
• (First) sort on Rating
• And then (secondly) on Hotel Name

(*b*) • Create a standard letter
• Insert fields from the database
• Mail merge

(*c*) (i) Any two from:
• Software has less features than stand alone packages
• Uses up more memory (than a single application)
• Parts of the integrated package would be redundant

(ii) Users only have to learn one HCI

(*d*) (i) A field that is calculated/includes a formula

(ii) Total Cost

3. (*a*) Any two from:
- All staff can access the same information at the same time
- All of the information can be kept up-to-date
- Staff can send information electronically (from one machine to another)
- Easy to communicate instead of sending pupils around school
- Pupil info easily and quickly collated
- Staff can access all info in school not just own department

(*b*) Any two from:
- To see the data stored about them
- To have incorrect/out of date data amended
- To seek compensation for damages caused from the storing of incorrect data

(*c*) Any two from:
- Files organised so easy to locate
- Different levels of access for different users
- Files in different directories can have the same names

(*d*) (i) A reference to all the features of the package which can be accessed while using the package

(ii) Command driven is fast as commands are entered quickly on the keyboard/user does not have to go through a series of menus

(iii) Menu driven is better for beginners who do not have to memorise the commands

(*e*) (i) Integrated package
Different parts of the package, word processor, spreadsheet and graphics parts are required
OR
Desktop Publishing package
Used to produce documents including text and graphics

(ii) Text which appears at the bottom of each page
AND ONE POINT FROM
- Which is only entered once but appears on all pages
- Is the same on all pages

(iii) A printer driver

(*f*) (i) Any two from:
- Easy to carry around
- Cheap/easy to create and/or distribute
- The software cannot be altered
- The CD-ROM has a high capacity

(ii) SIMILARITY – one from
- Look the same
- Both read (and written to) by a laser
- Used by similar drives
- Similar storage capacities

DIFFERENCE – one from
- CD-ROM cannot be written to
- Can look different (colour)

4. (*a*) (i) Copy

(ii) Absolute referencing – the reference to the cell containing the handicap (B3) must remain constant

Relative referencing – the reference to the cell in column C must change so that the correct gross score is used for each row

(*b*) (i) Data changed in one part of the package will be automatically changed in the other part

(ii) The chart will be automatically updated as data is entered

(*c*) (i) The computer is capable of doing several tasks (running several programs) at the same time

(ii) Any idea of having two programs open at the same time

(*d*) (i) ASCII code/binary

(ii) Any one from:
- Characters that make the computer do a specific task
- Characters do not produce a printable character

(iii) Any two from:
- Printing
- Moving around her spreadsheet
- Accessing menus
- Tab
- Return
- Cursor keys

5. (*a*) (i) A (computerised) simulation/model that behaves (or looks) like real life/3-dimensional

(ii) Any one from:
- Headset
- Dataglove
- Position tracker
- Helmet
- Visor
- Monitor

(*b*) Any two from:
- All moving parts of robots need to have guards to stop humans being injured by them
- Robots need to be fitted with bump or proximity sensors so that they can stop when a collision happens or is about to happen
- Robots should move slowly to minimise damage caused by collision
- Robots fitted with sirens/flashing lights to warn humans
- Safety clothing
- Emergency stop button

(*c*) Any one from:
- The number of axes/planes of movement that the robot has
- The number of joints the robot has

Computing Studies
Credit Level 2003 (cont.)

5. continued

    (d)   (i) A language specially designed to control/operate a robot/machine

          (ii) Any one from:
- They are easier to read and write as they use commands written in English
- They are problem oriented
- They are portable
- They are easily edited

         (iii) Interpreter alerts programmer of errors as soon as they are written
Compiled programs saved in machine code run quicker/takes up less memory

    (e) Closed loop
The system reacts to feedback/signals from sensors

    (f) Any two from the following:
- Robots can work all the time without breaks
- Robots are more accurate so goods are of better, more consistent quality
- Robots work faster than people
- Less wastage of time/materials

Computing Studies
General Level 2004

1. (a) 1. Centred
              2. Emboldened

    (b) (i) Changing the size
        (ii) Any two from:
- Graphic has been copied and pasted
- Graphic has been moved
- Border has been removed

    (c) Scanner, Digital Camera, or Digital Video Camera

    (d) (i) Any one from:
- Copies are produced very fast
- Quiet in use
- High standard of output
- Any other acceptable answer

        (ii) Any one from:
- Expensive to buy
- Toner expensive
- Colour not available

    (e) Any one from:
- Ink cost
- Paper cost
- Toner cost
- Electricity cost
- Any other running cost

    (f) (i) A list of instructions that the computer follows, OR an executable file.
        (ii) A file that the user or program has created.

2. (a) Search and replace

    (b) A paragraph, which is saved and can be used many times.

    (c) Any two from:
- Change the top and bottom margins
- Change the left and right margins
- Change the line length
- Change the line spacing
- Change the kerning
- Change the paper size
- Change the font size
- Shrink to fit
- Change the font

    (d) Lessons within the program which will take you step by step through the program.

    (e) Any two from:
- Ease of transfer of data
- Common HCI
- May be cheaper to buy than separate packages
- May require less memory than separate packages
- May require less backing storage than separate packages

2. (*f*) (i) Human Computer Interface
  (ii) Any one from:
    • Ease of using a mouse
    • No need to remember commands
    • Ease of transferring data between windows
    • Ease of clicking on icons
    • More user friendly
    • Easier for beginners

(*g*) (i) Data can be entered directly to a desktop
  OR
  There is no need to rewrite a story
  OR
  It's portable
  (ii) Liquid Crystal Display
  (iii) Handwriting Recognition

3. (*a*) Add/create a field/column with appropriate heading (eg Charge) OR enter data

(*b*) (i) Search/find/query on transport field equals yes
  (ii) Sort on event

(*c*) Any two from:
  • Can communicate with other user on the network
  • Can access own files on any machine on the network
  • Can share printers
  • Can share software/data/files
  • Any other acceptable answer

(*d*) Any two from:
  • Password protection
  • Changing access rights
  • Locks on doors
  • Only copy on removable media
  • Locks on machines
  • Encryption
  • Firewalls

(*e*) (i) Any one from:
    • Can work on the file at home
    • Can use on computers not on the network
    • Can keep as a backup
    • Save space on hard disks
  (ii) Any one from:
    • Can work on file from any station on the network
    • Confident that a backup is made regularly
    • Data can be shared
    • Large files can be stored
    • Faster access
    • Larger capacity
    • You don't need a disk – everything is there already

4. (*a*) (i) 1. F3
      2. E3
  (ii) =SUM(F2:F6)
      =F2+F3+F4+F5+F6
      Not = SUM(F2+F3+F4+F5+F6)

4. (*b*) Insert a row, enter data, replicate formula, update the "total" formula.

(*c*) 1. Select the cells
  2. Change to currency format

(*d*) Change column width
  OR
  Change font size

5. (*a*) (i) The last digit
  (ii) To ensure that the data has been entered correctly/validation
  (iii) A calculation based on the other digits

(*b*) (i) Any one from:
    • No need to carry money/cheque book
    • Money cannot be stolen or lost
    • Customer can get cashback
    • Itemised billing
  (ii) Any one from:
    • The funds are in the store account
    • No need to go to the bank to deposit cheques
    • Less money in the till to balance
    • Less money is lost if the shop is robbed
    • Less chance of fraud
    • Can give cashback
    • Guaranteed payment

(*c*) A station without processing power or without backing store

(*d*) 1. Computer is free during the day to deal with other business
  2. Once program and data are loaded little human intervention is needed.

(*e*) (i) A file which holds data to update/change to the master file.
  (ii) Changes to stock levels
    OR
    Changes to staff records
    OR
    New stock
    OR
    Any other suitable answer

(*f*) Advantage – Any one from:
    • The computer system will not allow access to a voice it does not recognise
    • No keyboard needed

  Disadvantage – Any one from:
    • Expensive to implement
    • Access may be banned if personnel has a cold
    • Voice of person allowed access may be taped

6. (*a*) Any two from:
    • Close off access to the rink
    • Sensors on the sweeper
    • Sirens or bells
    • Flashing lights etc

(*b*) (i) Response is immediate
    OR
    Output immediately follows processing
  (ii) Batch processing
    OR
    Interactive processing

Computing Studies
General Level 2004 (cont.)

6. continued

   (c) (i) Any two from:
- English-like words make it easier to write code
- Programs are portable
- Any other suitable answer

     (ii) Any one of:
- The sweeper program would have to be altered
- The sweeper would have to be reprogrammed
- A signal sent from device to the computer
- Any other suitable answer

   (d) (i) Sensor: Device which measures or monitors its surroundings
Feedback: Signal sent from the device/sensor to the computer.

     (ii) Closed loop system

   (e) Any two from:
- Controlling input devices
- Controlling output devices
- Managing memory
- Managing backing store
- Any other suitable answer

   (f) Any two from:
- No need to employ a person to do the job
- Machines can never be off sick
- Machines don't make mistakes
- Any other suitable answer

Computing Studies
Credit Level 2004

1. (a) (i) A letter that is used many times
Is always the same except for personal details

     (ii) Mail merge

   (b) (i) 150 bytes

     (ii) 1.44Mb
= 1.44 * 1024 * 1024
= 1509949.44 bytes
Number of records
= 1509949.44/150
= 10066
(Only accept whole numbers of records.)

OR

1.44Mb
= 1.44 * 1000 * 1000
= 1440000 bytes
Number of records
= 1440000/150
= 9600

   (c) (i) Data Protection Act

     (ii) Any two from:
- (The customer) can check the data held about them
- (The customer) can have any incorrect data amended
- (The customer) can claim compensation for any damages caused by inaccurate data.

   (d) Any two from:
- The spell checker has a dictionary/memory of words
- It goes through a document highlighting words that are not in the dictionary
- It offers alternative words to those it highlights

   (e) Printer driver

2. (a) (i) A sensor/thermistor/thermostat/transducer

     (ii) Closed loop

     (iii) Real time/not interactive

     (iv) Changed (from analogue) to digital

   (b) (i) Any two from:
- Software cannot be changed accidentally (or maliciously)
- Software loads much quicker
- Memory is retained when the system is switched off
- Software immediately available at switch on

     (ii) Any one from:
- Software is difficult to update
- This is a very expensive method

   (c) Any one from:
- The language is written specifically for the task
- The language contains special commands for the job

2. (*d*) Any one from:
- Computer is more accurate
- Computer is checking the temperature all of the time
- You do not have to pay a wage
- Any other suitable answer

3. (*a*) (i) Copy
   (ii) Relative referencing – The cell references in D14 have to change (according to the new column).

(*b*) A = IF
      B = D14 <= B15

(*c*) Dynamic

(*d*) (i) Hardware – Modem
      Software
      - Dial-up software
      - Internet browser
      - Communications (accept named) software
      - Any suitable software.
   (ii) Many users can use the Internet site at the same time
   (iii) Any two from:
      - Internet updates are done straight away – no delay
      - The Post could be lost
      - The Internet is cheaper than posting
      - Don't need to buy stamps
      - Post slower than Internet
      - More convenient than having to go out
      - Don't need printout

4. (*a*) (i) Check Digit
   (ii) Stock Level
      OR
      Total value of stock
   (iii) Random access
      - Fast access to the database is required so that the checkout runs quickly
      - Changes made to database frequently and easily

(*b*) (Complex) Search/Query/Find/Filter
      Product Manufacturer = "Gimballs" AND
      Product Price > £0.50

(*c*) A field that contains a calculation or a formula

(*d*) (i) All three of:
      - The customer's card is scanned/swiped/read (and their bank is contacted)
      - The bank sends a message back to authorise the payment
      - The transaction is made and the money is transferred (later)
   (ii) Any one from:
      - Faster than paying by cheque
      - No need to carry large amounts of cash
      - Customers receive detailed statement at the end of the month
      - It's safer
      - Any other suitable reason

(*e*) A terminal away from the processor/computer/mainframe/server

5. (*a*) Any one from:
- A high level language uses recognisable (English language) words
- A low level language program only works on the type of machine it is written on
- A high level language program is portable/easy to read/understand/debug and modify
- Any other suitable answer

(*b*) (i) Interpreter
      - (It translates one line at a time,) highlighting any errors/Easy to edit mistakes
   (ii) Assembler

(*c*) (i) Portable software can be used by many different **types** of computer system
      Different platforms/different OS
   (ii) The software can be bought by more customers
      No need to write different versions

(*d*) Nobody can (legally) copy/sell Rhona's programs

(*e*) Any two from:
- Make regular
- Back up copies
- And keep them in a safe place (away from the original)

(*f*) (i) Menu-driven
      - User does not have to learn commands
      - Commands cannot be mistyped
      OR
      Command driven with a suitable reason
   (ii) Any two from:
      - WIMP/GUI Interface
      - Inclusion of on-line help
      - Inclusion of an on-line tutorial
      - Any other suitable answer

6. (*a*) (i) Control Unit/CU
   (ii) Arithmetic and Logic Unit (ALU)

(*b*) (i) Any one from:
      - Main memory
      - RAM
      - cache
   (ii) ROM

(*c*) The processor selects hardware devices for different tasks
      At different times

(*d*) Input – any one from:
- Scanner
- Digital (video) camera
- Microphone
- Video Capture Card
- Webcam
- Graphics tablet
- Any other suitable answer
Output – any one from:
- Speakers
- High Resolution Monitor
- Any other suitable answer

Computing Studies
Credit Level 2004 (cont.)

6. continued

    (e) (i) Any two from:
- CD-ROM has much larger capacity
- You cannot change the contents of the CD-ROM
- CD-ROM less easily damaged
- Not all machines have floppy disk drive
- Any other suitable answer

       (ii) Memory management – Places the file in main memory/RAM
OR
File Management – Locates the files on the CD-ROM and Input/Output control
OR
Error Reporting – If a problem occurs, problem is reported to the users
OR
Command Language Interpreter/HCI – Takes user input to find the file
OR
Any other operating system task with suitable explanation

Computing Studies
General Level 2005

1. (a) No. The Data Protection Act prevents this from happening/this is not allowed/it is illegal

    (b) Complex search or implication of complex search/on fields house equals Bardowie/and year equals first/Print out result of search

    (c) Add/Create a record for him

    (d) Password/physical security/encryption/firewall

    (e) Local Area Network

    (f) *Any two of*
- Ability to choose from menus
- Have icons to choose from rather than typing in commands eg printing
- Able to use the mouse for input rather than the keyboard
- user friendly

    (g) *Any two of*
- Toner/ink
- maintenance
- paper
- electricity

    (h) Backup copy

2. (a) (i) Search and replace/find and change
       (ii) Search for Mrs Smith and replace it with Mrs Smythe

    (b) A paragraph of text which is saved and can be used many times

    (c) Add Smythe to the dictionary, also accept Ignore All or just Ignore or word list

    (d) Resize, Scale (Any Notion of changing size) Rotate or notion of it changing angle

    (e) (highlight) one paragraph and cut it then paste it into correct position
Accept Cut and Paste, Drag and Drop, Select and Drag, Copy and Paste provided extra paragraph is cut

    (f) (i) Word processing (Program)
       (ii) Database/Graphics Package/spreadsheet

    (g) By the use of ASCII or a binary (code) for each letter or 1s and 0s

3. (a) B4+C4+D4 or SUM(B4:D4) or SUM(B4..D4)

    (b) E4-F4

    (c) Highlight all approproiate figures and change to currency

    (d) Add/Insert a column

    (e) Software made up of separate parts (with an indication of different applications)
Software containing database, spreadsheet, word processing, graphics

    (f) this makes it quicker/easier to learn

3. (g) Loads the data file into the computer
Checks to see which key has been pressed

(h) (A chart is easier to read) than a set of figures/presented better and easier to understand/easier to compare/more visual

(i) Introduction Session - Online Tutorial
Making a column wider whilst using the program - Online Help

(j) *Any two of*
- Clear
- good quality printout
- quieter
- faster printing
- more ppm (pages per minute)

4. (a) *Any two of*
- similar to English
- require translation into machine code
- use standard arithmetic operators
- problem orientated
- portable plus easier to edit
- easier to understand

(b) The computer's own language or language made up of binary numbers
Series of 1s and 0s

(c) pixels

(d) (i) Microphone
(ii) So that the computer can perform pattern matching and recognise her words.
So that the computer gets a chance to interpret the words/can understand her
(Any notion that the computer recognises the input and that this must be accurate)
(iii) The voice recognition package only has a limited dictionary of words which it has learnt
Notion of limited dictionary

(e) (i) Laptop, palmtop, tablet (Any portable system)
(ii) It is portable, don't need to plug it in (Any notion of portability)

5. (a) *Any two of*
- robots are more accurate than humans
- save money on wages
- to become more competitive
- fine tune production process and get rid of redundant actions
- faster than humans
- more efficient with reason
- less reject components being made because of constant standard
- safety - less danger to humans of such things as spray painting
- not enough skilled humans

(b) (Grid of) magnet/magnetic wires and a sensor which follows these underground wires
Programmed map and the route is entered remotely and followed by the robot

5. (c) *Any one of*
- fencing off
- flashing light
- warning beep
- posters
- protective clothing
- bumper sensor
- proximity sensor

(d) (i) Real time
(ii) Glue will be faulty if the temperature is too hot or too cold (accept answer which gives notion of immediacy)

(e) (i) Closed loop
(ii) (Sensors) provide feedback which is then responded to by a change of control signals if necessary

(f) Analogue

(g) (i) Hard Disk
(ii) Large storage capacity
or direct access
or random access
or fast access
or large amount of memory

6. (a) (i) Batch processing
(ii) Notion of batching orders together or for the idea of automatic processing with no human intervention

(b) Uniform Size, Range check
Quantity/Type check, etc

(c) Transaction

(d) (i) Magnetic Ink Character Recognition
(ii) *Any one of*
- it is difficult to forge
- require translation into machine code
- more accurate processing
- it is human and machine readable

(e) Advantage: no travelling expenses
or more flexible working hours
Disadvantage: Less sociable
or will not be a success if you are not disciplined

(f) *Any one of*
- bad for the environment
- makes people angry with most of it ending up in the bin
- generates a lot of paper
- idea of "spam" (take up memory, introduce viruses, clogs up in-box)

Computing Studies
Credit Level 2005

1. (a) (i) • 160 (bytes)
     (ii) • 160 × 10000 = 1,600,000 bytes
         • (number of Kbs =)1600000/1024 = 1562·5
           (OR 1600000/1000 = 1600)
         • (number of Mbs =)1562·5/1024 = ~1·5
           (OR 1600/1000 = 1·6)
         • number of disks = 2

     (b) (i) *Any two of*
         • obtain and process the data fairly and lawfully
         • register the purposes for which they hold it
         • not use or disclose the information in a way contrary to these purposes
         • only hold information that's adequate, relevant and not excessive for the purposes
         • only hold accurate information and, where necessary, keep it up-to-date
         • don't keep the information any longer than necessary
         • allow individuals access to their information and, where appropriate, correct or erase the information
         • take appropriate security measures
      (ii) *Any two of*
         • to check to see if an organisation holds information about you
         • to see a copy of the information
         • to have any incorrect or out-of-date information amended
         • to claim compensation for damages due to misuse

     (c) (i) *Any two of*
         • same letter sent to many people—idea of fixed part
         • the only difference being the personal details—idea of variable part
      (ii) *Any three of*
         • complex search/query/find/filter—or notion of complex search
         • Network = Talkfone or contains Talkfone
         • (AND) Town = Newtown or contains Newtown
      (iii) mailmerge

2. (a) *Any one of*
         • computer is more accurate
         • checks water level at all times
         • saves money on wages
         • any suitable (eg safety aspects, efficiency with reason)

     (b) (i) sensor
         (ii) changed (from analogue) to digital
        (iii) closed loop

2. (c) (i) *Any one of*
         • language written specifically for task
         • language more suited to controlling system
         • contains specialised commands
      (ii) *Any two of*
         • loads faster
         • less liable to corruption (virus)
         • cannot be (easily) erased accidentally or deliberately
         • permanent storage medium

     (d) B. ISPs generally provide e-mail accounts
        D. Communications and Browser software is needed for Internet access

     (e) (i) *Any two of*
         • performs all the arithmetical operations OR calculations
         • performs all logical operations OR comparisons on any data passed to the processor
      (ii) *Any one of*
         • supervises the execution of the program instructions inside the processor
         • controls timing of events in processor

3. (a) (i) copy
        (ii) relative

     (b) (i) =IF D4>10; D4*B1; 0
         (ii) B1
       (iii) *Any one of*
         • cell protection
         • lock cells
         • use password

     (c) (i) *Any one of*
         • style or formatting applied to the cell or contents
         • appearance of contents of cell
         • characteristics of cell, eg width, colour etc
      (ii) *Any one of*
         • alter to currency (NOT money or £s)
         • any appropriate style or format, eg bold, underline

     (d) Dynamic, with valid reason
         • table (in report) would be updated (automatically)
         • table always changes
          If Static, then need valid reason for both marks
         • permanent record required for each month

4. (a) *Any one of*
         • computed field
         • calculated field

     (b) (i) *Any one of*
         • ensures that data is valid
         • to check that the data has been entered correctly (NOT data is correct!)
      (ii) from (any of) the other digits in the code

4. (c) *Any two of*
- random access
- fast access times required OR immediate access/retrieval needed

(d)
- most recent backup is child
- child becomes parent, parent becomes grandparent
- idea of rotation—grandparent deleted and new child saved in place (accept clear diagram)

(e) (i) *Any one of*
- terminal away from the processor
- terminal which is not located near the computer processing the data
- terminal with no independent processing power

(ii) • many people (can use the computer)
- at the same time/at the one time

(iii) Customers will be buying train tickets from different call-centre employees at the same time

(f) *Any three of*
- card details entered (scanned or numbers input)
- bank contacted
- payment authorised
- transaction made/money transferred

(g) *Any two of*
- change resolution (dots per inch)
- change font
- increase size of icons/fonts/cursor
- change colour scheme
- adjust brightness/contrast
- (any suitable—must be software based)

5. (a) *Any two of*
- more specialised/sophisticated functions
- saves money—no redundant packages
- less memory needed to run—only one application
- less backing storage needed

(b) *Any two of*
- (size of) main memory
- correct version of OS (OS may be incompatible)
- (adequate) processor speed
- (sufficient) backing storage

(c) Copyright (Design & Patents) Act

(d) (i) *Any one of*
- information/tips (given by the program)
- quick reference guide (while using computer)
- (looking up information)

(ii) lessons/exercises on features/step by step guide

5. (d) continued

(iii) *Any one of*
- can be used by different types of computer system
- can be used by different computer platforms

(iv) *Any two of*
- large storage capacity
- not easily damaged
- cannot alter software
- cost—cheap medium
- wide availability of CD drives
- easily mass produced

(e) (i) *Any two of*
- number of different programs
- running at the same time/concurrently

(ii) *Any two of*
- processor needs to be able to select hardware devices for tasks
- devices must be connected and disconnected as different resources are required
- devices allocated according to requirements of programs

(iii) *Any two of*
- (main memory organised as) separate storage locations
- (each having) unique/individual address